On Board the USS *Mason*

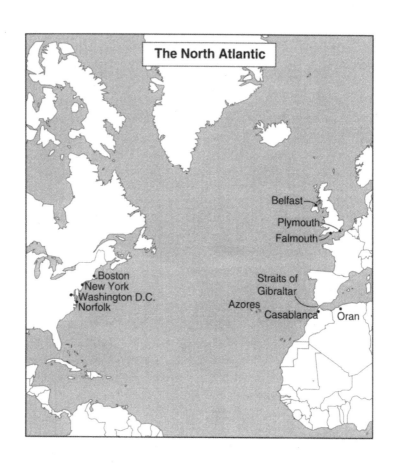

The North Atlantic

Belfast

Plymouth

Falmouth

Boston
New York
Washington D.C.
Norfolk

Straits of
Gibraltar

Azores

Casablanca

Oran

On Board the USS *Mason*

The World War II Diary of
James A. Dunn

Edited and with an Introduction by
Mansel G. Blackford

With a Historical Introduction by
John Sibley Butler

Trillium, an imprint of
The Ohio State University Press
Columbus

Library of Congress Cataloging-in-Publication Data
Names: Dunn, James A., 1913– author. | Blackford, Mansel G., 1944– editor. |
Butler, John S. (John Sibley), writer of introduction.
Title: On board the USS Mason : the World War II diary of James A. Dunn /
edited and with introduction by Mansel G. Blackford ; with a historical introduction
by John Sibley Butler.
Other titles: On board the U.S.S. Mason
Description: Columbus : Trillium, an imprint of The Ohio State University Press,
[2016] | Includes bibliographical references and index.
Identifiers: LCCN 2016031381 | ISBN 9780814206997 (pbk. ; alk. paper) |
ISBN 0814206999 (pbk. ; alk. paper)
Subjects: LCSH: Dunn, James A., 1913—Diaries. | Mason (Destroyer escort) |
World War, 1939–1945—Naval operations, American. | African American sailors—
Diaries. | United States. Navy—Biography.
Classification: LCC D774.M36 D86 2016 | DDC 940.54/5973092 [B]—dc23
LC record available at https://lccn.loc.gov/2016031381

Cover design by Andrew Brozyna
Text design by John Delaine
Type set in ITC Galliard and Gill Sans

9 8 7 6 5 4 3 2 1

I would like to dedicate my diary to Heywood Pullen, the past Grandmaster of the State of Ohio's Prince Hall Grand Lodge (Masons); to Frederick Kelley, the present Grandmaster; and to members of the Gloria lodge number 89; and also to Robin Rankin, Barbara Rowell, Jackie Stewart, and Sandy Brown.

And to my beloved son, James Jr., and my daughter, Muriel.

—James A. Dunn

Contents

Historical Introduction

It is a pleasure to introduce readers to this diary, which reveals the innermost feelings and experiences of someone who served in the navy during World War II. Scholars of military organizations understand that diaries are rich sources of data that can supplement the strong historical documentation of the military experience in America. In this diary, readers have the opportunity to see service in the U.S. Navy through the eyes of a person of African descent. The purpose of this introduction is to provide a background of the history of military service to the country by black Americans, so that the reader will better understand the experiences of James A. Dunn as his diary unfolds.

When James Dunn was born in 1913, black Americans already had a tradition of service to their country which reached back over two hundred years. Indeed, blacks have established themselves in all conflicts and wars throughout America's history. They represent one of the few racial or ethnic groups in the country who can make this historical claim. Despite this fact, the history of their service to country is wrapped around the reality of racial discrimination and racism.

Before the Revolutionary War, the British American colonies faced two basic military threats: the first from the armed forces of Spain and France, and the second from the Indian tribes native to the new world. Each colony devised its own plans for the utilization of manpower, manpower that included both free blacks and slaves. These men, who served in the militia for each colony, were expected to take up arms during conflicts, especially those involving the Indian population.[1]

In 1715 the colony of Virginia had a conflict with the Yamasee

Indian tribe, and black militiamen were called to serve in order to secure the victory. As early as 1639 the General Assembly of Virginia passed an act that not only allowed slaves to participate in the militia but also tied service to freedom. In addition, the act provided for compensation to the owner for a slave who received freedom. The act noted, in part:

> Whereas, it is necessary for the safety of this colony in case of actual invasions, to have the assistance of our trusty slaves to assist us against our enemies, and it being reasonable that the said slave should be rewarded for the good service they may do us, be it therefore enacted . . . that if any slave shall, in actual invasion, kill or take one or more of our enemies, and the same shall prove by any white person to be done by him, shall, for his reward, at the charge of the public have and enjoy his freedom . . . ; and the master or owner of such slave shall be paid and satisfied by the public . . . ; and if any of said slaves happen to be killed in actual service of province by the enemy, then the master or owner shall be paid and satisfied for him.[2]

Although all of the English colonies provided provisions for using both free and slave manpower during times of conflict, they tended to rely more on free blacks than on slaves. Officials of the North Carolina colony, during an Indian conflict fomented by the Spanish, thought of issuing weapons to slaves but decided that "there must be great caution used, lest our slaves when arm'[d] might become our masters."[3]

During this time, the developing armed forces of the "United States" tried to follow policies adopted by the state militias. The navy banned "Negroes or Mulatoes"; the marine corps followed a similar pattern but permitted the use of black fifers and drummers to attract crowds during periods of recruitment.[4]

On October 2, 1750, the Boston *Gazette* carried an advertisement seeking a slave who had run away from his master. The ad read: "Ran away from his master William Brown Framingham . . .

a black fellow, about 27 years of age, named Crispas; six feet two inches high, short curled hair, his knees nearer together than common; had on a light color'd bearskin coat. . . ." Although ten pounds were offered as a reward for the slave, he was never captured.[5]

Twenty years later, this runaway slave, who was called Crispus Attucks, appeared in print again when he became the first person to die in the American Revolution. A Boston newspaper called the conflict with British soldiers the "Boston Massacre" and described the event as follows: "Monday evening . . . several soldiers of the 29th regiment were abusive in the street, with their cutlasses, striking a number of persons. . . . A group of citizens, apparently led by a tall, robust man with a dark face, appeared on the scene. There came down a number from Jackson's corner, crying damn, they dare, we are not afraid of them; one of these people, the dark man with a long cordwood stick, threw himself in, and made a blow at the officer . . . crying kill the dogs, knock them over. The black man was shot."[6]

When the "mob" that had gathered in Boston to attack the British troops was brought to trial, all of the evidence pointed to Attucks; newspaper reports singled him out, in praise or blame, as the shaper of the event. John Adams, one of the lawyers for the Crown and later to become the second president of the United States, laid all the blame on Attucks. He believed that he was one of a motley rabble of boys, Negroes and mulattos, Irish teagues and jack-tars.[7]

Although Attucks was the first to shed his blood in an event that proved a rallying point for the colonists, when the Revolutionary War began, General George Washington's headquarters issued four orders forbidding black enlistment in the Continental army.

The British forces, on the other hand, offered blacks their freedom if they would join the side of the Crown. In many cases, blacks did join the English side. As Benjamin Quarles points out in *The Negro in the American Revolution,* "The black soldier in the

Revolutionary War can best be understood by realizing that his major loyalty was not to a place nor a people, but to a principle. Insofar as he had freedom of choice, he was likely to join the side that made him the quickest and best offer in terms of those 'unalienable rights' of which Mr. Jefferson had spoken. Whoever invoked the image of liberty, be he American or British, could count on a ready response from blacks."[8]

But the British were not completely successful in their bid for black soldiers. When news of their plans reached General Washington, he issued an order authorizing recruiting officers to accept free blacks. In a letter to the Continental Congress, he wrote: "It has been presented to me, that the free Negroes, who have served in the past, are very dissatisfied at being discarded. As it is to be apprehended, that they may seek employment in the Ministerial Army, I have presumed to depart from the resolution respecting them, and have given license for their being enlisted. If this is disapproved by Congress, I will put a stop to it."[9] Congress did not disapprove of Washington's actions, and blacks were allowed to enlist officially in the Continental army; only Georgia and South Carolina refused black enlistment.

It has been estimated that over five thousand blacks served in the Revolutionary War. Although the ranks were integrated, the typical black soldier was a private, and he tended to lack an official identity. Often his records were under no specific name. He was carried on the rolls as "A Negro man," or "Negro by name," or "A Negro name not Known."[10] As the war developed, not only did blacks enlist on their own, but many slaves served in place of their masters. The seven brigades of Washington's army averaged fifty-four blacks each. "Rhode Island, which early felt the pinch of Congress' demands upon her for men, proposed to raise a battalion of blacks in 1778, with freedom the bounty for slave enlistees, the master receiving a maximum of one-hundred twenty pounds for each slave. Massachusetts had one separate black company, recruited in Boston, which called itself the 'Massoit Guards' and another, flying a flag bearing a pine tree, a buck, and the initials 'J.H. & G.W.,' called the 'Bucks of America.'"[11]

The situation of blacks in the Continental navy is not well documented. It is known, however, that the navy, like the other services, was not segregated. The records show that blacks were entered on the ships' books without any distinction—again, much like the other services. It also shows that black pilots, because of their knowledge of coastal waters, were in great demand on ships sailing the Eastern Seaboard.[12]

When the shot heard around the world was fired, black soldiers were on the scene. At Concord and at Lexington, black and white men stood shoulder to shoulder, experiencing racial contact they had never known before. Blacks were present at the battles of Saratoga, Red Bank, Princeton, Savannah, Monmouth, Bunker Hill, White Plains, and Long Island. On the sea, the navy for the first time allowed the participation of blacks in its ranks.

But the defeat of British forces that secured white liberties also removed the need to allow blacks the freedom to fight, or their freedom from bondage. The ideology of war, the promises of freedom by the army, were replaced by the conservatism of the constitutional era. The racial aftermath of the war was summarized by John Greenleaf Whittier, poet laureate of antislavery, at a July 4th celebration in 1874:

The return of the festival of our national independence has called our attention to a matter which has been carefully kept out of sight by orators and toast-drinkers. We allude to the participation of colored men in the great struggle for freedom. When we see a whole nation doing honor to the memories of one class of its defenders, to the total neglect of another class, who happen to be darker complexion, we cannot forgo the satisfaction of inviting notice to certain historical facts which, for the last half century, have been quietly elbowed aside. . . . Of the services and suffering of the colored soldiers of the revolution, no attempt has been made, to our knowledge, to preserve a record. They have no historian. With here and there exception, they all passed away, and only some faint tradition of their campaigns under Washington, Greene, and Lafayette, and of their cruising under Decatur and Barry, lingers among their descendants. Yet enough is known to show that the free colored men of the United States bore their full proportion of the sacrifices and trials of the Revolutionary War.[13]

The War of 1812 was fought largely by the navy, and the use of black seamen continued. They were aboard American naval ships in all ratings and formed about one-sixth of total naval personnel. About one-tenth of the crews that sailed the Upper Lakes, with Colonel George Crogham at Mackinac, in 1814, were blacks.[14]

When the War of 1812 started, however, there was controversy over the use of black troops. The policy makers of the army were suspicious about the loyalty of blacks to the United States, and the view was prevalent that blacks should not be enlisted in the armed forces. But General Andrew Jackson, acting much like Washington had done during the Revolutionary War, issued a proclamation to the free black inhabitants of Louisiana: "To every noblehearted, generous freeman of color volunteering to serve during the present contest with Great Britain . . . there will be paid the same bounty, in money and lands, now received by the white soldiers of the United States—one hundred twenty-four dollars in money, and one hundred and sixty acres of land." In issuing the proclamation, he characterized the existing policy that excluded blacks as "mistaken." Following his decisive victory over the British in January 1815, in which some eight hundred blacks participated, Jackson was lavish in his praise for the black men who had joined him.[15]

Despite Jackson's support, in 1823 the attorney general of the United States stated that "it was not the intention of Congress to incorporate Negroes and people of colour with the Army any more than with the Militia." Throughout the first half of the nineteenth century, the army and navy forbade the enlistment of black soldiers.

At the time of the Civil War, the practice of using blacks to alleviate manpower shortages during a conflict and then rejecting them afterward was again in effect. By late 1862 and continuing through 1863, white volunteering in the Union forces had all but come to a standstill. The Conscription Act of March 1863 was met with numerous disturbances and riots. The growing opposition to military service by white men forced the Union to turn to blacks, who were thus allowed to join the army to fight against their former owners.[16]

War Department order G0143, issued in May of 1863, permitted black enlistment. During the war nearly 180,000 blacks fought on the side of the Union. In the army they were formed into separate units designated United States Coloured Troops. Blacks fought in pivotal battles and won fourteen congressional medals of honor.[17]

The navy allowed black enlistment as early as September 1861. A slave pilot, Robert Smalls, ran the Confederate gunboat *Planter* out of Charleston in May 1862, delivering it to a Union port. He was appointed a pilot of the USS *Keokuk* during the battle at Fort Sumter and was promoted to captain because of his gallant and meritorious conduct there. He later returned to the *Planter* and served as its captain throughout the war.

Although there were individuals such as Robert Smalls, the navy followed the lead of the army and developed a system of segregation. A few sailors, left over from an integrated navy, served as petty officers and other ranks, but the 30,000 black navy volunteers were assigned to the messman branch. Thus in a real sense, blacks in the navy had only restricted opportunities during the Civil War.[18]

After the Civil War, the War Department took the position that the enlistment of blacks could not be permanent but should be a "peculiarity of the volunteer service." Under this policy, blacks were not authorized for the regular service.[19] Blacks who chose to stay in the service were placed into the Ninth and Tenth Cavalry. These soldiers, called "Buffalo Soldiers" because their hair reminded the Indians of the buffalo, had as their major task the control of hostile Indians on the Great Plains for almost twenty years. These cavalry soldiers were placed under white officers and received some of the worst equipment, assignments, and camps. Nevertheless, their record of service was excellent as they patrolled the West and interacted with prejudiced whites in frontier towns.[20]

In June 1898 blacks responded to the call to arms to fight in the Spanish-American War. Black troops joined with Teddy Roosevelt, as "Rough Riders," in the victorious charge up San Juan Hill. In a communiqué, Roosevelt wrote, "I want no better men beside me in battle than these colored troops showed themselves to be." At El Caney, black troops won high praise for bravery when under heavy fire they stormed a stone fort defended by Spanish troops.[21]

World War I was fought at a time when race relations in the country were at a low ebb. President Woodrow Wilson had ordered federal employees in Washington, D.C., segregated. In 1915 there were sixty-nine lynchings of blacks. When the United States declared war on Germany in 1917, black leaders urged blacks to support Wilson's call to "make the world safe for democracy." At the same time, however, Frank Park, a representative from Georgia, introduced a bill to make it unlawful to appoint blacks to the rank of either commissioned or noncommissioned officer. Despite this hostile attitude, blacks responded to the call, and more than 200,000 served overseas. They were divided into four black regiments of the regular army.

After the war, the 92nd Division found itself immersed in controversy. In contrast to other all-black units, the overall performance of this division was called into question. A comparison of the experiences of the 92nd and of the also all-black 93rd Division—and of the attitudes of those who commanded them—will help us understand how the reputations of the two divisions came to differ so widely.

Both the 92nd and 93rd were sent to France, and both were led by black officers in junior grades and by white officers in senior grades. Under French officers, the 93rd fought with honor and distinction. The French had such a high regard for the 93rd that it was awarded the croix de guerre. The French even requested that the United States send to France all black units that could be spared.[22]

The history of the 92nd, however, was very different. Even while it was still in training, black leaders became suspicious of the army's intentions toward the division. W. E. B. Du Bois, writing in the *Crisis,* the official newspaper of the NAACP, maintained that the division was headed for failure unless the army improved its training, equipment, and staffing.

When the 92nd reached France, it was commanded by white American officers. Reports by these officers charged that black troops in the 92nd were cowardly, stupid, and sexually brutal. And despite the outstanding record of the 93rd, the 92nd became the unit that stereotyped black soldiers; this was the unit that represented the black man in uniform. General Robert Bullard, expressing the view of the War Department, said, "If you need combat soldiers, don't put your time upon Negroes."[23]

But perhaps the most degrading attitude toward blacks came from General Pershing's headquarters. In a memo addressed to the French military mission entitled "Secret Information Concerning Black Troops," Pershing wrote: "We cannot deal with them [blacks] on the same plane as with white American officers without deeply wounding the latter. We must not eat with them, must not shake hands or seek to meet with them outside the requirements of military service. . . . We must not commend too highly the black American troops. . . . Make a point of keeping the native cantonment population from spoiling the Negroes."[24] As a final insult, black troops were rushed back to the United States within four months of the Armistice with a parting exhortation to return without causing any disturbances.

Black veterans returned to face a struggle no less fierce than the one overseas: the "red summer" of 1919. More than seventy blacks were lynched during the first year after the Armistice. Ten black soldiers, some still in uniform, were lynched.[25]

Between World Wars I and II, the army remained segregated and adopted a policy, the quota system, that kept the number of blacks in the army proportionate to the total population. By 1940 there were only five thousand men in all-black units, and only five black officers.

As America prepared to enter World War II, many members of the black population bitterly remembered the experience of black soldiers in World War I. A. Philip Randolph, a labor leader and civil rights activist, called for a march on Washington to end segregation in both civilian and military life: "We call upon you to fight for jobs in National Defense. . . . We call upon you to struggle for the integration of Negroes in the Armed Forces. . . . This is the hour of crisis. . . . To American Negroes, it is the denial of jobs in Governmental defense projects. It is widespread Jim-Crowism in the Armed Forces of the nation."[26]

Such prewar demonstrations would not have any effect until after the war. During World War II, the services remained segregated. There were four black army regiments, and more than a million black men and women served in the armed forces.[27] Among those who served was James A. Dunn, the author of this diary.

James Dunn would see many changes take place that would have a lasting effect on the participation of blacks in all services of the military. As a navy man, of course, he would be particularly affected by the policies adopted by the navy.

In 1940 the Selected Service Law was passed, calling to service all American citizens. Frank Knox, then secretary of the navy, declared that blacks could be accepted in the navy only as mess attendants. When inquiries were made about this policy, the navy issued a statement that "the policy of not enlisting men of the colored race for any branch of the naval service but the messman's branch was adopted to meet the best interests of general ship efficiency. . . . This policy not only serves the best interests of the Navy and the country, but serves as well the best interests of Negroes themselves."[28]

This policy drew pages of criticism from the black press. In the 1940 issue of the *Crisis* magazine, a columnist wrote:

> We hope American Negro citizens appreciate fully what this policy means to them. There is more to this than standing on the deck of a warship in a white uniform. To be stigmatized by being denied the opportunity of serving one's country in full combat service in the Navy is humiliating enough. But the real danger and greater injustice is to deny a tenth of the citizens of this country any benefit whatsoever from the billions of dollars spent on our Navy. Our taxes help keep up the Naval Academy at Annapolis where our boys may not attend. They help to maintain the numerous naval bases, Navy Yards, and naval air bases from which we are excluded. Of the great sums that go for wages and salaries we get but a few pennies. The training in numerous trades and skills which thousands of whites receive and use later in civilian life is not for us! The health care, the character building, the training in efficiency, the travel and education—all at the expense of the taxpayers—are for whites only! This is the price we pay for being classified as a race, as mess attendants only! At the same time we're supposed to be able to appreciate what our white fellow citizens declare to be the "vast difference" between American Democracy and Hitlerism.[29]

In 1942 the navy reversed its policy of recruiting blacks only as messmen and accepted them as volunteers in the navy and the Coast Guard. But black and white sailors would be trained in separate, segregated units. On June 1, 1942, 277 men arrived at Great Lakes Naval Training Center for basic training. Men were also trained at the Hampton Institute in Virginia.

The navy of James A. Dunn would also see the first group of black officers introduced into its ranks. Even when the navy was integrated in earlier wars, there had been no black officers. In January 1944 sixteen black sailors reported to Great Lakes Training Center in Illinois. When they completed their training, they became the first active-duty black line officers in the navy—146 years after the Navy Department was established, in 1798.[30]

Despite these advances, there was still much racism in the navy. In October of 1943 twelve black navy Seabees stationed in the West Indies were told by their commanding officer to talk about racial conditions at an open meeting. The men were told that the meeting would be off the record, and black personnel complained that although 80 percent of the battalion was black, not one of them was rated above second-class petty officer, while all of the remaining 20 percent, who were white, were rated higher in rank. The next day the black sailors were discharged as "undesirable" and unfit for service. They were also charged with "gripping." After an appeal, they were given honorable discharges.[31]

The black press continued to push for the equal treatment of black personnel in the service. As a result of the activities of the press and other civil activities, on February 2, 1944, the navy published a pamphlet entitled "A Guide to the Command of Negro Personnel." It promised that everyone in the navy would be judged on individual performance rather than race: "The Navy accepts no theories of racial differences in inborn ability, but expects that every man wearing its uniform be trained and used in accordance with his maximum individual capacity on the basis of individual performance."[32]

After the pamphlet was issued, the navy announced that two ships, a patrol craft and a destroyer escort, would be manned with mostly black crews under white officers. Experienced white petty officers were to serve as instructors on the ships, but as soon as the black sailors reached a level of competence at sea, the white officers were to be transferred and replaced by blacks. On March 20, 1944, the destroyer escort USS *Mason* was placed in commission, with 160 blacks and 44 whites as crew. In April a 173-foot submarine chaser, the USS *PC-1264*, was commissioned. This ship had a crew of fifty-three blacks and nine whites and was commanded by four whites.[33] The USS *Mason*, of course, was James Dunn's ship.

During the course of the war, a general military policy was established that was designed to increase the number of black officers in the army; develop the Tuskegee Institute program, which concentrated on combat pilots; deal with negative racial comments, which were so much a part of American society and the military; and integrate black soldiers into the overall structure of all military branches.[34]

In order to deal with the reality of racial inequality, in 1945 the army convened a special board of officers. This board was headed by Lieutenant General Alvan C. Gillem, and its conclusions would go down in history as the Gillem Report. The board was convinced that the army should expand, not limit, opportunities for blacks. During deliberations the board placed on the table two blueprints for dealing with the problem: the army could treat a black soldier like any other citizen and assign him solely on the basis of ability and the army's needs, with no attempt to segregate on the basis of race or color; or it could attempt to create a separate Negro army with the same variety of units and requiring the same range of skills as an army for whites.[35]

The Gillem board decided on the latter plan. Segregation was to be maintained. Thus, if black soldiers were to be used according to their abilities, black units would have to be created that in general conformed to white units. Although the board focused on segregation, it also recommended experimental, mixed-race units. The board recommended six major policy points:

1. Negro units in the postwar army should in general conform to white units.
2. Qualified Negroes should be used in overall head units.
3. A staff group in Army Headquarters and in every major command should be created to supervise racial policy and practice.

4. Periodic surveys of manpower should be made to determine positions that Negroes could fill.
5. Reenlistment should be denied to the professional private.
6. There should be experimental groupings of Negro and white units.[36]

From these points one can see that the board concentrated on the overall implementation of a policy of systematic racial segregation. The board also imposed a 10 percent quota on the number of black troops that could participate in the army.

When the board reported to President Truman, they reported to what was called the President's Committee. This committee doubted that the Gillem board's recommendations could achieve racial equality in the postwar army through its proposed system of "separate but equal." The committee also questioned the 10 percent quota for black soldiers. After reviewing the report, the committee sent back a recommendation to the Gillem board including the following points:

1. Open up all army jobs to qualified personnel without regard to race or color.
2. Open up all army schools to qualified personnel without regard to race or color.
3. Rescind the policy restricting Negro assignments to racial units and overhead installations, and assign all army personnel according to individual ability and army need.
4. Abolish the racial quota.[37]

In addition to the Gillem board, in 1949 the secretary of the army, Gordon Gray, appointed a board of general officers to look at the utilization of black troops. This board was under the leadership of Lieutenant General Stephen J. Chamberlin, and its entire deliberations were published as the Chamberlin Report. The final document issued by this board also called for a continued segregation of black and white troops and a 10 percent quota for black troops.

Although the army defended segregation, Truman took the president's prerogative and signed Executive Order 9381: "It is the declared policy of the President of the United States that there shall be equality of treatment and opportunity for all persons in the Armed Forces. This policy shall be put into effect as rapidly as possible, having due regard to the time required to effectuate any necessary changes without impairing efficiency or morale."[38] Truman also established the Fahy Committee to pursue equal treatment for military personnel. Under the guidance of this committee, the army was in the midst of integrating some training camps when the Korean conflict materialized.[39]

The military in World War II provided the setting for several now-classic studies in the field of race relations. These studies would also influence the court cases that decided the future of segregation in civilian society. One such study was done by Samuel Stouffer and associates,[40] who were interested in looking at the impact of racial contact on the attitudes of black and white military personnel. The researchers expected that, under certain conditions, the more contact different races had with one another, the more positive their attitudes would be. This was expected to be true when *(a)* an authority strongly sanctions interaction, *(b)* there are commonly shared goals, *(c)* the contact is between individuals of equal status, and *(d)* interaction between individuals is cooperative and prolonged, involving a wide range of activities.[41]

Using the military setting as a laboratory, Stouffer found that it was indeed true that the more contact blacks and whites had with one another, the more positive they felt about each other. This study was used to sanction the total integration of the military, and it was also cited during the deliberations of the celebrated *Brown vs. Board of Education* case, which outlawed racial segregation in public schools.[42]

Although there was some integration of troops during the latter part of World War II, it took the Korean War to completely alter the segregation policies of the military. The need for combat soldiers was high, which resulted in bringing blacks out of support units—where they had for the most part been concentrated in the two world wars—and assigning them to combat units. Integrated units performed well in combat. As integration in Korea became standard, it was noted that there was no difference in the fighting abilities of blacks and whites.[43] For the first time since the Revolutionary War, blacks and whites fought together in integrated units.

In Korea there were 73 all-white companies, 16 all-black companies, and 139 integrated companies. As the conflict proceeded, the military set up a baseline study of the integration of blacks into the military. This study, known as Project Clear, used questionnaires that measured the feelings and attitudes of black and white troops. The data show that there were black troops who thought they would get a "better break" in integrated units and there were whites who felt that blacks were not capable of being combat soldiers.[44] But Project Clear also reinforced the conclusions reported by Stouffer in *The American Soldier* stressing the importance of racial contact, under certain conditions, for the development of positive racial attitudes. In the Project Clear documentation, the general finding was that white troops at first resented the idea of integration but that this resentment quickly disappeared. At present there appears to be no evidence of any impairment of unit morale where blacks have been completely integrated.[45]

The peace that followed the Korean conflict witnessed an increase in efforts by the military to ensure a policy of integration. The cold war era, from 1952 to 1965, saw a continuing improvement in race relations in military service, especially in the army. By the middle of the 1950s, the military was viewed by many commentators as being engaged in a revolution, the result of allowing all Americans to defend their country:

> Tell one of the generals . . . that he and his brother brass are staging a social revolution among the half-million Americans posted to duty . . . and he will profess the greatest astonishment. "Why, we

are just implementing a routine directive of the Army in an ordinary war," he will reply, as though it were hardly worth mentioning. It may be a paradox that the staff planners of the . . . Army . . . refuse to recognize the dimensions of the task they are performing—and that the very matter-of-factness of their approach has been a major factor in its success thus far. Yet, the fact remains that this "ordinary implementation of a routine directive" does add up to a revolution in race relations and appears to be setting a pattern not yet equaled elsewhere in our Armed Forces or anywhere in our country.[46]

This "revolution in race relations" led one writer to claim that "the U.S. Army has solved the Negro integration problem still plaguing much of the rest of the nation."[47] The optimism of this period is also noted by the fact that Pentagon news releases told of southern restaurants being open to Negro soldiers in uniform (even though Jim Crow laws were prevalent), and of white southern families inviting Negro servicemen home for dinner or for a weekend. There were reports that even in Brownsville, Texas, where in August 1906 black troops were accused of shooting whites in a raid, the First Presbyterian Church invited Negroes from a nearby base to attend any or all of its services, "right along with whites." The attitudes of black soldiers reflected the temper of the times. As one black sergeant noted, "We've got one Army over here now. We don't have two—one white and one black any more." In fact, the point could be strongly made that the level of race consciousness among blacks (at least overtly) was very low, if it existed at all. The black soldier conceived of himself as an American fighting man, and not as a black fighting man.[48]

By the time of the Vietnam War, black troops were so well integrated into the army that Charles Moskos, the most distinguished scholar on the subject of race in the military, noted that "taken within the historical context of the 'right to fight,' voiced by Negro organizations with reference to the segregated military of World

War II, the black soldier's current overrepresentation in combat arms might be construed as a kind of ironic step forward."[49]

The Vietnam War witnessed the highest proportion of black participation in war or conflict in American history. In 1968 alone, 70,000 black servicemen were employed in the war; thousands served in the years before and after 1968. But blacks were overrepresented in combat arms and thus were overrepresented among those who died from combat.

When the conflict Desert Shield/Desert Storm took place in 1990–91, the racial integration of the military was complete. Over 500,000 American troops, 24 percent of whom were black, were sent to the Persian Gulf. For the army, the figure was 30 percent black.[50]

Operation Restore Hope in Somalia was the first major deployment of American troops to an African nation. The operation was successful, and the black troops served with distinction.

The diary of James A. Dunn is an interesting slice of the black experience in uniform. As one reads the diary, one gains a deeper understanding of the experiences, fears, patriotism, and overall feelings of blacks who have served their country since before the Revolutionary War.

—John Sibley Butler

Notes

1. Bernard C. Nalty and Morris J. MacGregor, *Blacks in the Military: Essential Documents* (Wilmington, Del.: Scholarly Resources, 1981), p. 1.

2. Ibid., p. 3.

3. Ibid., p. 1.

4. Bernard C. Nalty, *Strength for the Fight: A History of Black Americans in the Military* (New York: Free Press, 1986), p. 20.

5. New York Graphic Society, in association with the Smithsonian Institute, *The Black Presence in the Era of the American Revolution* (New

York: Smithsonian Institute Press, 1973), p. 6.

6. Ibid., pp. 7–8.

7. Ibid., pp. 8–9.

8. Benjamin Quarles, *The Negro in the American Revolution* (Chapel Hill, N.C.: University of North Carolina Press, 1961).

9. USAEUR Race Relations School, "Black Soldier, a Compendium" (Washington, D.C.: Department of Defense, 1972), p. 1.

10. "Lists and Returns of Connecticut Men in the American Revolutionary War, 1715–1782," Connecticut Historical Society, Collection 12 (1909), 59, 80, 81, 183.

11. USAEUR Race Relations School, "Black Soldier," p. 2.

12. Dennis D. Nelson, *The Integration of the Negro into the U.S. Navy* (New York: Farrar, Straus & Young, 1951), pp. 1–2.

13. New York Graphic Society, *Black Presence*, p. 41.

14. Nelson, *Integration of the Negro*, p. 2.

15. For a discussion, see Johnny S. Butler, *Inequality in the Military: The Black Experience* (Saratoga, Calif.: Century Twenty One, 1975).

16. Nelson, *Integration of the Negro*, p. 4.

17. Butler, *Inequality in the Military*, p. 31.

18. Nelson, *Integration of the Negro*, p. 8.

19. Jack D. Foner, *The United States Soldier: Between Two Wars* (New York: Humanities Press, 1970), p. 127.

20. For an excellent discussion, see William H. Leckie, *The Buffalo Soldiers* (Norman: University of Oklahoma Press, 1967).

21. Butler, *Inequality in the Military*, p. 32.

22. Stephen Ambrose, *The Military and American Society* (New York: Free Press, 1972), p. 196.

23. Butler, *Inequality in the Military*, p. 35.

24. Richard J. Stillman, *Integration of the Negro in the U.S. Armed Forces* (New York: Praeger, 1968), p. 9.

25. Stokely Carmichael and Charles Hamilton, *Black Power: The Politics of Liberation in America* (New York: Vintage Books, 1967), p. 26.

26. August Mier, *Black Protest Thought in the Twentieth Century* (New York: Bobbs-Merrill, 1969), p. 221.

27. Ibid., p. 33.

28. Nelson, *Integration of the Negro*, pp. 12–13.

29. Ibid., p. 14.

30. Paul Stillwell, ed., *The Golden Thirteen* (Annapolis, Md.: Naval Institute Press, 1993), p. xxvi.

31. Jack D. Foner, *Blacks and the Military in American History* (New York: Praeger, 1974), p. 168.

32. Ibid., p. 170.

33. Foner, *Blacks and the Military,* p. 170.

34. For a discussion, see Ulysses Lee, *The Employment of Negro Troops* (Washington, D.C.: Center of Military History of the United States Army, 1963).

35. Nalty and MacGregor, *Blacks in the Military,* p. 287.

36. Ibid., p. 288.

37. Ibid., p. 292.

38. John P. Davis, *The American Negro Reference Book* (Englewood Cliffs, N.J.: Prentice-Hall, 1971), p. 652.

39. Charles C. Moskos, *The American Enlisted Man* (New York: Russell Sage, 1971), p. 111.

40. Samuel Stouffer, et al., *The American Soldier* (Princeton, N.J.: Princeton University Press, 1949).

41. For a discussion, see John Sibley Butler, "Race Relations in the Military," in *The Military: More Than Just a Job?* ed. Charles C. Moskos and Frank R. Wood (Washington, D.C.: Pergamon-Brassey's, 1988), pp. 115–27.

42. Ibid.

43. Moskos, *The American Enlisted Man,* p. 111.

44. For a discussion, see Leo Bogart, ed., *Project Clear: Social Research and the Desegregation of the United States Army* (1969; New Brunswick, N.J.: Transaction Publishers, 1992).

45. Ibid.

46. Ernest Leiser, "For Negroes, It's a New Army Now," *Saturday Evening Post,* December 13, 1952, p. 26.

47. Lee Nicholas, *Breakthrough on the Color Front* (New York: Random House, 1954), p. 221.

48. Butler, *Inequality in the Military,* p. 39.

49. Moskos, *The American Enlisted Man,* p. 116.

50. General Accounting Office, "Operation Desert Storm: Race and Gender Comparison of Deployed Forces with All Active Duty Forces," June 25, 1992.

Preface

In the late winter of 1995 Mary Pat Kelly, a freelance writer and filmmaker in New York City, published a book, *Proudly We Served: The Men of the USS "Mason,"* with the Naval Institute Press. A destroyer escort, the USS *Mason* (DE 529) escorted convoys of merchant ships to the United Kingdom and North Africa during the closing years of World War II. What set the *Mason* apart from other naval vessels was her crew: most were African American. In fact, the *Mason* was the only sizable warship during the war to employ African Americans in positions other than that of cook or mess mate. The ship had white officers. While Kelly was researching her book, she contacted me for information about my father, William M. Blackford, who was the captain of the *Mason* during all of the ship's convoy duties in 1944 and 1945. I was happy to give her what materials I had, mainly letters my father wrote home while on board ship. Kelly introduced me to the surviving crew members, all she could locate, at a gathering in her apartment in New York City in the winter of 1994. I owe Mary Pat Kelly my heartfelt thanks for getting me together with the men of the *Mason*.

We all met again at a special ceremony hosted by the navy in Washington, D.C., in February 1995. The purpose was twofold: to launch Kelly's book, just published, and to honor the men who had served on the USS *Mason*. In a moving ceremony, the secretary of the navy presented surviving crew members with letters of commendation for "meritorious service" and "unrelenting determination and steadfast devotion to duty" under extremely difficult conditions on one particular convoy (for further discussion of this event and the honoring of the crew, see under Dunn's diary entry for October 19, 1944).

Preface

Accounts of the navy's award ceremony were carried in newspapers nationwide. One person who had not been at the ceremony and who had not known about Kelly's book was James A. Dunn, who had served as one of the *Mason*'s four signalmen. A resident of Columbus, Ohio, Dunn read about the publication of Kelly's book and the ceremony in Washington in a local newspaper. Having learned that I was a professor of history at The Ohio State University, he then telephoned me. Dunn and I met on several occasions to discuss his wartime experiences. During one of these interviews, he mentioned that he had kept a diary recording his actions and thoughts during his service. That diary is reproduced here, with only light editing on my part.

My deepest debt is, of course, to James A. Dunn. I want to thank him for allowing the publication of his diary and for participating in interviews with me. I would also like to thank crew members of the USS *Mason* for repeatedly discussing their experiences with me. Special thanks are due James W. Graham, who was in the communications division on the *Mason*. In the early 1970s Graham organized the USS *Mason* Association to preserve the ship's history. In several conversations he helped me understand the ship's operations.

A number of my colleagues in the Department of History at The Ohio State University have provided valuable advice: Professors John C. Burnham, William C. Childs, John F. Guilmartin, Susan M. Hartmann, Allan R. Millett, Stephanie J. Shaw, and Warren R. Van Tine. Anthony Milburn, a doctoral candidate in history at Ohio State, also provided useful suggestions. I would like to thank as well Charlotte Dihoff, the acting director of the Ohio State University Press, and William M. McBride, the outside reviewer for the press, for careful readings of the diary in manuscript form. David Stefacek, a doctoral candidate in history, helped me type out Dunn's diary from the original handwritten volumes.

—Mansel G. Blackford

Preface for the Paperback Edition

On Board the USS Mason: *The World War II Diary of James A. Dunn* tells the story of the lives of the men on a destroyer escort during World War II, as seen through the eyes of one of the ship's sailors, Signalman James A. Dunn. This volume reprints Dunn's daily diary. Dunn and the other men of the *Mason* made ten crossings of the Atlantic, protecting merchantmen and troopships from attacks by German submarines and shepherding ships in convoys through horrific weather conditions, including a full-force hurricane.

What set the *Mason* apart from other naval vessels of that time was her crew: most of the crew members were African Americans. In fact, the *Mason* was unique. She was the only sizeable, ocean-going warship during World War II to employ African Americans in positions other than that of cook or messmate. The men of the *Mason* were, thus, like the much-better-known Tuskegee airmen in the army airforce. They were pioneers in creating new places for African Americans in the armed forces of the United States. However, there was an important difference: while the airmen had black officers, the sailors had white ones. My father, William M. Blackford, served as the captain of the *Mason* during all of that ship's crossings of the Atlantic.

My father was not a civil-rights advocate, but he did want to run a good navy ship. For him that meant handling the *Mason* well and making it possible for his men to get ahead in their ranks. When some white chief petty officers objected to serving with African American crew members, he had the petty officers transferred to other ships. When white sailors on navy docks in Miami, Florida, refused to handle the *Mason*'s lines, he had them disciplined.

When a crowd (or possibly a mob) of white dock workers advanced in a menacing fashion on the *Mason* in Norfolk, Virginia, he had the ship's guns trained on that group, which then dissolved. Crew members respected the way my father and the other white officers stood up for them when necessary. My father's ship-handling abilities also impressed the men of the *Mason*. One crew member later spoke for many when he stated, "Our captain, he treated us like men." Another said that they would follow their captain to hell and back, if need be. Several noted that my father handled the *Mason* smoothly as if she were "his Buick." Asked by a newspaper reporter in 1973 if he thought his experiences were different from those of the officers of other naval vessels because of the nature of his crew members, Blackford replied, "Different? No, not really." But, of course, they were. Not all in the navy wanted the *Mason* to succeed. Detractors disparaged the *Mason* as "Eleanor's folly" and the "nigger ship." Eleanor Roosevelt championed the *Mason* with her husband, President Franklin D. Roosevelt, against the reluctance of the Secretary of the Navy Frank Knox.

For me, learning about the *Mason,* mainly from surviving crew members, was a profoundly moving experience. That I would have that opportunity was most unlikely. I owe heartfelt thanks to Mary Pat Kelly, a freelance writer and filmmaker in New York City, for first bringing me together with the men of the *Mason.* In the late winter of 1995, Kelly published an account of the history of the *Mason* titled *Proudly We Served: The Men of the USS* Mason, with the Naval Institute Press in Annapolis, using as the words for her book's title those suggested by the sailors of the ship. She later produced a one-hour documentary film and then a first-run film about the men and their experiences on board the *Mason.* While Kelly was researching her book, she contacted me for information about my father. As it had happened, my mother had recently passed away (my father had died four years before), and, with my sister, I had just finished going through their house in Seattle to prepare it for sale. In several old, musty cartons in a corner of the basement, I found letters my father had written home during World War II, along with various navy reports. I was happy to supply Kelly with the materials I had for use in her writing. In turn, Kelly introduced me to about a dozen surviving crew members, all that she could locate, at a gathering in her apartment in New York City in the winter of 1994. That get-together, which lasted for several days, was quite an affair for me.

Two particular developments still stand out from our initial meeting. First, at the various lunches and dinners, the former sailors took me aside to tell me anecdotes about "the captain" or "the boss"; they never said "your father." My father had never told me much about his wartime experiences, but I learned about some of them from his crewmen: from ramming what they thought was a German submarine in the Straits of Gibraltar (it turned out to probably be a half-sunken barge) to having lively picnics on beaches at Oran in North Africa (where flies were everywhere). Second, navy officers had mounted a museum display about the *Mason* on board an aircraft carrier temporarily docked in New York City, which I toured with my father's former crewmen. For me, the highlight of that visit came when present-day African American sailors going through the display recognized the World War II men of the *Mason,* high-fived them, and asked question after question about their experiences. I simply stepped back, watched, and listened. The young men received a personal tutorial from their seniors, then in their seventies and eighties, about what the navy and American society had been like some fifty years before. We left the display about ninety minutes later.

Additional get-togethers followed. In February 1995, we all convened in Washington, DC, to help launch Kelly's book, which had just been published, and to honor the men who had served on the *Mason.* In a truly moving ceremony, Secretary of the Navy John Dalton presented surviving crew members who could be located with long-overdue letters of commendation for "meritorious service" and "unrelenting determination and steadfast devotion to duty" under extremely difficult conditions on one particular convoy. Dalton was referring to heroic efforts on the parts of the sailors in saving part of a convoy during a hurricane in the fall of 1944. Not all of the surviving sailors had been found ahead of time, but the event was well-publicized. During it, several additional crewmembers emerged from the audience for the first time, leading to much backslapping and hugging on the part of their former shipmates. Some had tears in their eyes. (For a fuller discussion of this navy event and the honoring of the crew, see Dunn's diary entry for October 19, 1944.)

I met with crew members for a final time in mid-April 2003 to participate in the commissioning of a brand new navy destroyer, the USS *Mason*, named after the World War II vessel. Once again, I learned more about my father and his ship's wartime experiences from the men, including the story of my father's dog, who somehow fell overboard into the Atlantic. The dog was rescued when the *Mason* reversed course and found him about five or ten miles to the rear, cold but doing a strong dog paddle. The major event of the commissioning came when the new warship "came alive," as the men and women of the *Mason*, uniformed in dress whites, raced to their battle stations and then stood at attention. Flags were hoisted on the destroyer, and her missile mounts rotated. For me, however, the high point came when I visited the sailors' mess room, appropriately named after my father, who always loved a good meal and drink.

While it was unlikely that I would get to know some of my father's crewmen, it was even less likely that I would edit and publish the diary of James A. Dunn. Living in Columbus, Ohio, where he worked and raised a son and daughter with his wife, Jane, Dunn had been out of touch with his former shipmates since the close of World War II. He had not known about Mary Pat Kelly's writing, nor about the navy's ceremony honoring the men of the *Mason*. That ceremony, however, made the national news, and Dunn read about it in a Columbus newspaper. Having moved to Columbus in 1972, I was a professor of history at The Ohio State University, and the newspaper report mentioned my name. A day after the article about the *Mason* ran in the newspaper, Dunn telephoned me in my office. We soon got together at his home, and he agreed that I could interview him about his experiences on board the *Mason* (I work in modern American history). Near the end of the last scheduled interview session I asked Dunn a question he could not answer; he responded that he would have to check his diary, previously unmentioned to me. He did so and then allowed me to look at the diary.

Fascinated, I borrowed the diary for several days, read it several times, and became convinced that it had a lot to say about wartime life in the mid-1940s. I thought that the diary should be published. Dunn agreed. James A. Dunn Jr., his son, later remembered: "My father always felt very strongly about their contribution to the service. They were expected to fail, to fall flat on their faces. That's what people wanted to happen. But they just wanted to show they were Americans and help protect the greatest country in the world. And they wanted to show that, given a chance, they could perform as well as anyone. They had a lot more to fight for." The men of the *Mason* fought for the double-V: victory over America's overseas enemies and victory over racism at home.

I offered to find an African American historian to edit his diary, but Dunn asked me to do so, saying, "I trusted the captain with my life. I can surely trust you with my diary." The diary is reproduced here, with only light editing on my part. Dunn was enthusiastic about having his diary published by The Ohio State University Press, for his family had ties to the university. He had attended Ohio State University football games as a young man and had even played in the university's massive stadium as a star high-school football quarterback. Decades later his daughter had earned a BA in social work at the university. (She died of cancer in the 1990s.) All royalties from sales of this volume go to Dunn's heirs.

Dunn went on to meet fellow crewmen at a reunion in May 1995, shortly before he died in 1996. His son, who accompanied him to the gathering, later recalled of his father: "He started planning for that trip in about March. He got a real kick out of being with the guys. It was really good for him." I felt honored to help reintroduce Dunn to his former crewmates, an exciting experience indeed. Understanding history can matter, can make a difference.

Many people helped make this published diary a reality. My deepest debt is, of course, to James A. Dunn. I want to thank him for allowing the publication of his diary and for participating in interviews with me. I would also like to thank other crew members of the USS *Mason* for repeatedly discussing their experiences with me. Special thanks are due to James W. Graham, who was in the communications division on the *Mason*. In the early 1970s, Graham organized the USS *Mason* Association to preserve the ship's history. In several very detailed conversations he helped me understand the ship's operations.

A number of my colleagues in the Department of History at The Ohio State University provided valuable advice: John C. Burnham, William C. Childs, John F. Guilmartin (now deceased), Susan M. Hartmann, Allan R. Millett, Stephanie J. Shaw, and Warren R. Van Tine. Anthony Milburn, a doctoral candidate in history at Ohio State, also offered useful suggestions. I would like to thank as well Charlotte Dihoff, the acting director of The Ohio State University Press who initially pushed for the publication of this diary, and William M. McBride, the outside reviewer for the Press, for careful readings of the diary in manuscript form. Finally, Tony Sanfilippo, the current director of The Ohio State University Press, has my thanks for making Dunn's diary available as a paperback.

—Mansel G. Blackford
2016

Introduction

Born in 1913 in a small town in a coal-mining area of West Virginia, James A. Dunn spent his childhood in Charleston, W.V., where his mother, Mary, worked as a domestic for a white family. When the father of that family, an engineer for a natural gas company, moved them to Columbus, Ohio, around 1926, Dunn and his mother came too. In Columbus Dunn attended the Clinton Heights School and Crestview Junior High School, located in what was then a predominantly white section of town. Of particular importance for his later work as a signalman was the emphasis placed on spelling in the schools Dunn attended. Dunn's teachers held many spelling bees, he remembers, pitting "one row [of students] against the other."

Dunn found time for nonacademic activities. In junior high he began playing organized sports, participating in speed ball (soccer), basketball, and track. Football, in which he would later star, was not offered then in Columbus junior high schools, but Dunn was able to play in a Saturday morning citywide league. He was captain of the team "Dubb's Cubs," which won the league championship one year. The elementary and junior high schools he attended were integrated; but Columbus, like many American cities at the time, was socially segregated. When going to movies in downtown theaters, Dunn remembers, African Americans "sat upstairs, way in the back."

Dunn began attending Central High, where he became the starting quarterback, the first African American quarterback on a high school football team in Columbus. In doing so, he learned skills—such as memorizing the signals in the playbook—that would later prove useful in his career in the navy. Central High

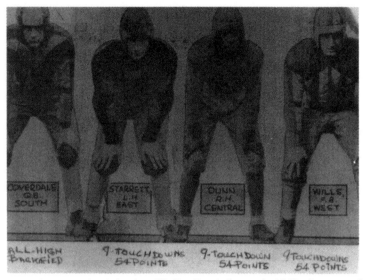

James Dunn on the Columbus All-City Football team in 1931. Courtesy of
James A. Dunn.

won the Columbus city championship in 1931, and football became a large part of Dunn's life. He enjoyed attending Ohio State
University football games and often sold "pinks," newspaper reports of the games that were sold on the street at the conclusion of
the game. He watched professional games between the Pittsburgh
Steelers and the Philadelphia Eagles at the Ohio State Fairground
in Columbus. It was, he says, a real treat to see the teams play, "just
like ice cream." Dunn studied the players to "pick up the moves—
how to pivot, how to give the man the leg." In high school he also
developed a love for the English language and did well academi-
cally. He recalls, "I loved English. I loved to read . . . the *Merchant
of Venice, Caesar.*"

Social segregation dogged Dunn in high school. In traveling to
away games, Central High's football team had difficulty finding
restaurants that would serve African Americans. His coaches, who

were white, always insisted on going to restaurants that would serve all the team members.

In his senior year in high school, Dunn moved back to Charleston with his mother when the family for whom she worked returned there. Here schools were segregated, and Dunn played football for Garnet High School, an all-black school. As quarterback, he took the team to the West Virginia state championship in 1933, and that year no other team scored against Garnet High. It was here that he met his future wife, Mary Jane Nowell, then a junior. A friend pointed her out to him one day, observing that she "was a nice-looking lady, but nobody seems to make headway with her." Dunn intended to try. To get to know her, he took the unusual step of enrolling in a cooking class she was taking at school. He talked with her in class, and "we picked it up from there."

After graduating from high school in 1934, Dunn enrolled at West Virginia State College, an African American school located in Charleston. Again, he played football. In return, he was given summer jobs in construction work on the campus. He attended college for two years, leaving in 1936—in part to marry Jane, which he did on July 12, 1937, and in part to get a job. Jane had a large family, and Dunn wanted to help support them. He found a job chipping and finishing steel at a nearby Carnegie Steel plant, a position he kept until he was drafted in 1942.

Dunn opted to go into the navy. "I didn't want to go into the army," he recalls, since he had heard from friends that the army training base at Fort Hood, Texas, had "foxholes with rattlesnakes."

African Americans had served in the navy from the American Revolution into the Progressive Era. During the Civil War about 30,000 African Americans had been sailors in the Union navy, about 30 percent of all of the enlisted men. But as part of the racism that swept across America in the late nineteenth and early twentieth centuries, African Americans were systematically excluded from the navy. When President Theodore Roosevelt sent his "Great White Fleet" of battleships around the world to show the American flag in 1907, few African Americans were on board. All but cooks and messmen had been forced to resign or to accept assignments on shore. Over the next few years, African Americans were forced out of other specialties in the navy by attrition.

The navy reversed its exclusionary policy in June 1942, influenced both by a shortage of men and by the prodding of African American leaders—Mary McLeod Bethune, A. Philip Randolph, W. E. B. Du Bois, and others—and of Eleanor Roosevelt, who often acted as the conscience for her husband. The navy thus began accepting African Americans for general service. But progress was slow. As late as February 1943, only 27,600 African Americans were in the navy: 19,000 in the stewards branch, 6,600 in general service (mostly in onshore facilities), and 2,000 as Sea Bees, construction workers. Ninety-eight percent of those in the navy were white.

Dunn trained at a segregated naval base, Camp Robert Smalls, named after an African American Civil War naval hero, just across the railroad tracks from the much larger Great Lakes Naval Training Center, for whites, near Chicago. Here he received sixteen weeks of basic "boot" training in classes taught by white officers. About three weeks into training the navy administered screening tests to determine what specialties the men would enter. As a result of the examinations, Dunn "was picked to be a signalman, because I was very good at spelling . . . and English."

In studying to become a signalman, Dunn learned both semaphore—how to signal with flags—and the Morse code, for use with signal lights. There were seventy-five flags and pennants, many of which were used in various combinations, that he had to be able to recognize instantly. In signaling with lights, he had to be able to send and receive messages at the rate of eighteen words per minute. (Signaling between ships was done whenever possible by flags and lights rather than by radio, because ships did not want to give away their positions to enemy vessels, which might intercept radio transmissions.) Dunn remembers his training at Camp Smalls as "tough." "We studied hard together. The instructors taught us hard."

Still, there was free time, and Dunn sometimes went into Chicago, where there was "good entertainment, clubs, baseball games, the Chicago Cubs." On the base he often played pick-up baseball games. When he completed his training at Camp Smalls, Dunn had a few days off, and, joined by his wife, he visited with friends he had made at the camp.

On graduating as a signalman, Dunn was assigned to work in the control tower at the harbor of Newport, Rhode Island. He and others in the tower directed the movement of ships into and out of Narragansett Bay. His wife joined him in Newport. Like many women during World War II, she worked in a defense plant, one making torpedoes—a job she would hold throughout the war, joining her husband whenever he was back in the United States on leave. Dunn remembers that at Newport he and Jane "had a wonderful time." In fact, he did not want to leave this posting.

But because of his superior performance at Newport, his chief recommended him for duty on the USS *Mason*. In the winter of 1943–44 Dunn went for about a week to Boston, where the ship was being constructed at the naval shipyard. Here he met the others assigned as crew members. Together, they took the train to a navy base at Norfolk, Virginia, for additional training.

At Norfolk Dunn and the others attended destroyer escort school. For Dunn that meant "learning everything about that particular ship" and receiving advanced training in signaling. Here, too, he and the other men began to coalesce as a ship's crew. They worked together to perform well in competition with the crews of other ships. That most assigned to the *Mason* were African American added a racial component to how they perceived their training. "We worked hard practicing to be ready, and we were," Dunn says. "We told each guy to study hard. We had to be twice as good, three times as good as anybody—better than the white boys." As a signalman, for him it was a matter of "memorize, work hard. You saw a flag and knew exactly what it was."

Norfolk and the naval base there were segregated, as Dunn and his fellow shipmates soon learned; one shipmate later characterized Norfolk as "Shit City" for African Americans. During one of their first nights the men were denied entrance through the front door of the base's movie theater; they were told to enter through the rear door. Thereupon, they telephoned their ship's officers. As Dunn recalls, the captain, Lt. Comdr. Blackford, came to the theater and "raised all kinds of hell. . . . He got excited. . . . He said 'this is a DE crew, my crew, and I want them in the theater. . . . You don't separate my boys.'" After about fifteen minutes the men were admitted, and from then on all enlisted men—black and white—used the same entrance. On another occasion, the men were returning to base after a night on the town. Told to move to the back of the trolley car, they refused. After arguing with the conductor, they threw him and the driver off, commandeered the trolley car, and drove it back to the base entrance themselves.

While the men were undergoing training, their ship was being built. The USS *Mason's* keel was laid on October 14, 1943, and she was launched on November 17, 1943. The *Mason,* commissioned in Boston on March 20, 1944, was one of hundreds of destroyer escorts—smaller cousins of fleet destroyers—mass produced to escort convoys of men and supplies to the Allies at the front. The *Mason* and her sister ships were to keep submarines away from the convoys of merchant ships, and to sink the submarines if possible. Some 289 feet long and 35 feet wide, the *Mason* displaced 1,140 tons and was capable of a speed of about 20 knots. She carried around six officers and two hundred men; the exact number varied with the trip. The *Mason* was armed with three 3"/50 guns (these guns fired shells 3 inches in diameter through barrels 150 inches long), nine 20 mm. automatic cannons, and one quad 1.1" antiaircraft gun. Her most important offensive weapons were her depth charges, which were rolled off racks on the stern of the ship or shot to the

The crew members admire their ship on commissioning day at the navy ship-yard in Boston. Courtesy of James Graham.

side of the ship by K-guns (mechanical catapults), and hedgehogs, projectiles shot off in a pattern in front of and to the sides of the ship, exploding under water.

What made the *Mason* different from almost every other ship in the navy during World War II was her crew: they were mainly African American. Initially, the crew was composed of 160 African Americans and 44 whites, but as African Americans advanced in their ratings, white crew members were transferred to other ships. The officers were white. The *Mason* was not originally intended to be manned by African Americans, but as an increasing number of African Americans completed naval training at Camp Smalls and then served well at onshore facilities and on coastal vessels, pressure mounted for African Americans to man an ocean-going warship. The *Mason* was chosen for the experiment. Although the officers selected for the ship were given the option of declining duty once the decision was made to man her with African Americans, all accepted their assignments. Only the smaller submarine chaser *PC-1264*, operating in the coastal waters of the United States and in the Caribbean, had a crew of similar composition: fifty-two African American and nine white enlisted men, again with white officers.

After commissioning, the *Mason* made a shakedown cruise to Bermuda for a final testing of men and equipment (particularly radar and sonar). This was the first trip at sea for most of her crew, including Dunn. "Finally, we got out to sea," recalls Dunn. "The crew was eager, and we worked hard and feverishly." For five weeks in April and May the *Mason* trained with other DEs and with American submarines to perfect antisubmarine warfare tactics. After some additional training in Casco Bay, Maine, she sailed in early June for Charleston to escort a convoy across the Atlantic to the United Kingdom.

What follows is James Dunn's day-to-day account of his life as a signalman on the USS *Mason*. Dunn wrote his diary during his spare time in two volumes given him by his wife, Jane. Such diaries are a rarity, for the navy (and the other armed services) forbade the keeping of diaries, fearful lest secret information fall into enemy hands. I have made only occasional and very minor editorial alterations in Dunn's diary in the interests of readability. Explanatory comments and additions are enclosed in brackets.

Dunn's diary chronicles the *Mason*'s wartime activities, from the first convoy to the final return to the United States. His diary captures the feeling and meaning of life on board with an immediacy not found in later accounts. Here are men in mortal danger attacking submarines and dealing with horrendous weather conditions on the North Atlantic. Here, at the other extreme, are bored men cooped up on a small ship on long, tedious convoys. Here are the joys of shore leaves, the daily life aboard ship—the duties, but also the pastimes that made shipboard life endurable. Here is what it meant to be an African American in a white navy in a segregated

Crew members undergo inspection before shore leave in Miami after a shake-down cruise. Courtesy of James Graham.

American society. But here, too, is a love story between James and his wife, since the diary includes entries written as if they were letters sent home to her.

In short, this is a personal story about an important incident in American history.

The First Negro Crew in the
History of the United States

USS *Mason*

DE 529

James A. Dunn

The *Mason* Hymn

We're the men of the USS *Mason*
And we're a darn good crew
We fight with a patriotic devotion
For our country brave and true

We're the men of the USS *Mason*
And we stand for liberty
Full of courage with our nation
We will fight to make it free

As a crew we are tough
And you know we've got the stuff
(Give us a chance and you will see)
We're the men of the USS *Mason*
And we stand for liberty!!!

—*A sailor aboard the USS* Mason

I

The First Crossing of the Atlantic

June 14–July 25, 1944

The USS Mason's *sea duty was not long in coming. Originally intended for deployment in the South Pacific, the destroyer escort had been painted in jungle camouflage. However, the Allied invasion of Western Europe on June 6, 1944, changed her assignment, and the ship began escorting her first convoy across the North Atlantic in mid-June 1944.*

By this time the German submarine menace was not as severe as it had been during the opening years of the war. Into 1943 German submarines sank more merchant ships than could be built, thereby imperiling Great Britain, which depended on the United States for aid. The nadir, from the Allies' point of view, came in November 1942, when 720,000 tons of shipping were lost to submarine attacks. Only in February 1943 did the construction of new ship tonnage exceed submarine sinkings for the first time, and only in the fall of that year did new ship construction permanently exceed sinkings. Several factors shifted the tide in favor of the Allies. Remembering its experience in World War I, the navy began grouping merchant ships in convoys protected by a growing number of escort vessels. Moreover, the warships, especially destroyer escorts like the Mason, *were provided with better submarine-detection equipment, including the most advanced models of radar and sonar. Also important was the provision of HF/DF (high-frequency direction finders, nicknamed "Huff-*

5

The USS *Mason* at harbor with her crew on deck. Courtesy of James Graham.

Duff") for escort vessels, beginning in the summer of 1942. These devices could find German submarines by intercepting radio transmissions. Finally, the Allies broke the German naval code, which enabled them to locate German submarine wolfpacks and to route convoys around them.

Still, even with advances in antisubmarine warfare, German submarines remained a danger. In June 1944 the German navy received new types of submarines equipped with snorkels. The snorkels were basically tubes extending above the water to carry air down into submarines running just below the surface, which permitted them to avoid detection by radar. By February 1945 the German submarine force rose to over 400 ships, its largest size during the war (these submarines were not especially effective in sinking merchant ships, however).

As the Mason *put to sea on the first of her ten crossings of the Atlantic, James Dunn was one of four signalmen on board. The signalmen sent and received messages from other ships—and occasionally from blimps and airplanes—through the use of flashing lights and flags. They used two lights sixteen inches in diameter, one on the port (left) side and one on the starboard (right) side of the ship. With these lights, Dunn explains, they could send signals "ten to fifteen miles, if it was nice and clear." They also had one twenty-four-inch light, mounted on a swivel, that was capable of sending signals even farther under good conditions. The signalmen used the lights to send messages "in the clear" by Morse code. But they also often used flags to send messages in code, especially if it was feared that submarines were near enough to intercept messages transmitted by the lights.*

Two signalmen were normally on duty on the signal bridge, one on the port and the other on the starboard side. Dunn usually worked on the port side. When a message was being received, the signalmen worked together, with one reading the message and the other writing it down. The men then sent the message by telephone to the main bridge, to the captain and the other officers. Dunn usually served alternate watches of four hours each—four hours on duty, followed by four hours off. "You couldn't get too much sleep," Dunn recalls, "it was tiring."

June 14, 1944

We are getting underway at 0340. Each man is on his special sea detail. Our ship and four other destroyer escorts are moving slowly out of Charleston, S.C., Harbor. None of the boys seems to really know what we are going to do. About 0600 we see some merchant ships coming out of port. Then we knew that the real stuff was here at last. We are to take a convoy across, destination still unknown. After taking all day to form the convoy, we finally shove off for our destination. Everything is going along fine so far.

[The officers shared the enthusiasm of the men for the "real stuff." In a letter of March 23, 1944, to his parents, the captain of the *Mason*, Lt. Comdr. Blackford, observed, "It feels pretty good to be back on a ship at last, especially a real warship. . . . I think that the crew is better than average and is developing some spirit. There has been a lot of bunk said about Negro crews. We can't see that they are any different from others if treated the same."]

June 15, 1944

It is a very beautiful morning and the sun is glistening on the ink blue water. One of the merchant ships in the convoy has lagged behind and one of the escorts dropped back with her. But the rest of the convoy continues to push on toward its destination. The convoy is very slow and we can't make very much time. Our ship is astern of the Commodore's ship and he is really a tough fellow. [The commodore was the officer in charge of the entire convoy.] All of the messages are sent to us by flashing light and in turn we transmit them to the other ships. We have one of the best communicating divisions in the group. In fact the crew as a whole are strictly on the ball. Late this evening we contacted two enemy subs but they didn't give us any trouble. The alarm was sounded and each man was at his battle station in about two minutes and ready for action. One-half hour later the all secure signal was given but we were told to wear life jackets while on watch. We have a colored war correspondent aboard and he has taken pictures of the boys doing their respective duties. They have now sounded taps and the ship has been darkened.

> [Dunn is referring here to Thomas W. Young, the first African American war correspondent allowed on a navy warship at sea. His family owned the *Norfolk Journal and Guide*. After the convoy had completed its journey, Young wrote the director of public relations of the navy about his impressions of the *Mason*: "The crew of the *Mason* wants to make good, and, from my observations, it is entirely capable of doing so. One fortunate circumstance, it seems to me, is the further fact that they have a thoroughly competent Commanding Officer who has won both the confidence and admiration of the men" {August 10, 1944, copy of letter in the possession of the editor}.]

The USS *Mason's* four signalmen (left to right): Gordon Buchanan, Lorenzo DuFau, William Jones, and James Dunn. Courtesy of James Graham.

June 16, 1944

It is now 0400 and I am on watch on the flying bridge. There are two of us on watch, William M. Jones and myself. Everything seems to be quiet and going along fine. It is reveille time and everybody is getting up for morning chow at 0545. All of the ships are accounted for and we steadily push on. At 0600 the general quarters is given and each man rushes to his battle station, because subs usually attack this time of morning. At 0630 the all secure was given and everyone resumed their regular duties. At 1955 P-time [Peter-time, i.e., the local time zone designated by the letter "P"] I received a message from the escort that stayed behind with the merchant vessel saying that she only had 945 gals. of fuel. So the message was transmitted to the Commodore. At 1045 P-time I was relieved from watch by DuFau [Lorenzo A. DuFau] and Buck [Gordon D. Buchanan]. I went down and had my morning chow.

9

After finishing I hit my sack and slept until noon chow. The rest of the boys and myself laid around on deck just about all afternoon. I went back on watch at 1845 P-time. We had pretty heavy traffic but we managed to receive and transmit all of our messages correctly. Everything is still going along smooth and we haven't had any trouble as yet. I came off of watch at 2300 P-time and began to read a book which is very interesting. Before I could finish it the ship was darkened for the night and most of us went to sleep.

June 17, 1944

My shipmates and I went back on watch at 0400 this morning until 0800. We had our morning chow and relaxed for a few minutes. Our one point one and three inch fifties were fired in gun practice this morning and now things are pretty quiet. I am getting in my sack at the present, because you need all of the sleep that you can get. I was awakened at noon to eat chow and then proceeded to finish my story. We stayed on the signal bridge just about all of the afternoon. The Commodore sent a hundred and eleven group message and Buck and DuFau took it without missing a word. So you can see just how our signal force reacts. Our quartermasters are just as good in doing their job. The boys have a lot of fun ribbing each other and all of us take it with a smile. Nothing unusual has happened today. We have been out to sea for five days. Of course we haven't hit the part which is infested with subs as yet. But it won't be long now.

[The message Dunn talks about here, consisting of 111 words, was unusually long. Dunn recalls how careful he and the other signalmen had to be in taking down such messages. They did not want to have to ask the sender to repeat a message, "because that slows up the operations." To have to ask for a repetition would also injure their pride.]

June 18, 1944

It is a very beautiful Sunday morning and this will be another hot and sultry day. The boys are getting a little restless from riding, because as I mentioned once before that the convoy is very slow. But I think that everyone will get used to it sooner or later. We really should sight land about Tuesday morning, at least we are hoping to. Nothing exciting has happened as yet and we are still lounging around on topside.

June 19, 1944

The usual things are going on aboard ship except that we are nearing our destination. And it is very hot. We have been getting some very good meals here of late. Most of the boys write their loved ones or play cards during the spare time. The end of the day has come.

June 20, 1944

Early this morning the Captain said that we would enter Bermuda harbor very soon. All of the divisions turned to and the ship was in good condition. Later we entered the harbor and anchored. This same morning a German sub had been captured and twenty Germans had been killed during the affray.

June 21, 1944

All of the boys are waiting for liberty to be granted and about eleven thirty it was announced over the P.A. system that liberty would come at 1230. Half of the crew went on liberty this afternoon and didn't get into Bermuda until about four o'clock and they had to return at six. But didn't very many return. Davis

[Eldred Bryan Davis] our most brilliant yeoman takes it upon himself to see who was late coming in then submits the names to the executive officer.

[Tensions developed among crew members as they sought to make a good impression and to advance in the navy. In a recent interview Dunn said that Davis, who was himself an African American, was "a 'good' boy, a shaky boy, a brown-noser." Davis "thought the captain was going to help him {but} the captain would not play it." Other crew members also remember Davis in a similar manner. One recalls that he was a "brown-noser." Davis had earned a B.A. in mathematics at the University of Pittsburgh in 1936 and worked in the federal government's Office of Emergency Management before entering the navy. Coming on board the *Mason* as a yeoman, second class, he eventually advanced in rating to chief petty officer.]

June 22, 1944

Things are just about the same aboard ship today. Most of the boys are trying to catch up on some of their back sleep including myself. Another liberty party shoved off today about 3:00 P.M. and they likewise did not return at six. So Mr. Davis put the entire group on report. He is trying to get his commission but it will never be done on this ship. Little does he realize that he might have to ask one of the boys for a favor some time or other.

June 23, 1944

We had reveille at 3:30 A.M. and we are ready to get underway. All of the men are at their stations and the anchor is hoisted and the USS Mason is on her way again. We picked up our convoy just outside of the harbor and proceeded southeastward. That evening about nine thirty our soundmen [sonar operators] picked up something and we were so sure that it was a sub but found later that it was a whale. We are now headed for another unknown destination which is said to be very dangerous.

June 24, 1944

We seem to be going along very smoothly today and the boys are getting a little more rest than usual. Every one is on the alert looking for any trouble which might confront them. A British seaman died last night on one of the convoy merchant vessels. He was buried at sea today around 12:00 o'clock noon. All of the DEs dipped their colors to render honors to him. We are still forging ahead to our unknown destination.

June 25, 1944

Today was a very nice Sunday. Things are still going along smoothly. One of the oilers dropped a pretty good distance behind the convoy and we had to go back and see what the trouble was. It had broken down and was about six hours behind the convoy. We decided to tow it for a while. Later another DE came back to see what had happened to both of us. It stayed with the oiler and we came back with the rest of the convoy. We only have four DEs with the convoy at the present. We received news from the war fronts from the war correspondent on our ship. And everything is going along fine once again.

> [The correspondent, Thomas Young, often mingled with the men, asking them about their jobs on the ship and talking with them about what he knew of war developments. He had, Dunn recalls, "the full run of the ship."]

June 26, 1944

Things are just about the same on this bright Monday morning. We are still forging ahead to our destination which is the Azores, right out from the coast of Africa and France. We are keeping a very keen lookout for enemy subs, because we have had several contacts in the two or three days. And I have scratched one more day off of the calendar.

June 27, 1944

This morning while standing beside the officer of the deck my shipmate noticed that the ships in the convoy were out of line and he changed course and went in the middle of the convoy. We sent a message by light telling the ships to close up. Later all of them were back in their regular positions. Everything went along smoothly until late this afternoon. We picked up a sub and began to look for a periscope but didn't have any luck. We are nearing the Azores and will probably run into a wolfpack. It is believed that the Germans have a submarine base somewhere near the Azores, but I think that we will give them a good going over if we should sight any of them. Another day has ended.

[The Azores, a group of nine islands in the North Atlantic, are a Portuguese territory and were neutral during World War II. But in October 1943 the Portuguese government began allowing the Allies to use the Azores.]

June 28, 1944

Jones and myself went on watch at 0400 this morning and everything was still OK. The other DE that stayed behind a couple of days ago had caught up with us and took its same position in the convoy. We were glad to see it back, because there were only four of us to protect the convoys. We haven't had any fresh water to bathe in for about six days. But some of the boys have taken salt water showers. This morning we thought that we had run across a sub. The gun crews were ready and we started to drop depth charges. But after making a run on it there was nothing there. But it won't be long now. All of the boys are taking it easy at the present just lounging about the deck. We received our daily news report from our Mason reporter and it was very interesting. After this the captain ordered all men to their battle stations, because we're expecting an attack by enemy submarines. We stood around for hours waiting for an attack but nothing happened. Our signal force was given five thirty-thirty Springfield rifles and four knives. We are ready for anything at any time. And the crew are very confident. And another day has gone by.

[The rifles and knives were issued in case of man-to-man combat. If a submarine surfaced close to the ship after being rammed or depth-charged, the *Mason's* large guns might not be able to be brought to bear on it, and the crew might have to fight Germans emerging from the hatch. Dunn recalls that the seamen on the *Mason* wanted to be prepared for such a fight at close quarters.]

June 29, 1944

Nothing of any importance happened today. We just followed our usual routine. But since we have passed the half way mark of our voyage, all of us are keeping our life jackets close by. The boys are just waiting for our first attack. It is really hell waiting and watching but we can't see anything. But the zero hour is near and all hell might burst out at one time. But you can bet your life that we will be in there pitching with all we have.

June 30, 1944

The per usual things went on today without any interference whatsoever. Our C-Division [communications division] keeps very busy trying to pick up enemy messages and code. Our lookouts are on the alert at all times. The captain is very cool when we contact an enemy submarine. He is so anxious to get one of them that he offers twenty five dollars and a special leave to the first man sighting the first German sub. Three German subs surfaced about eighteen miles from us but nothing happened. We think that they are just waiting for a chance to attack.

July 1, 1944

We have been to sea just about a month and the boys are holding up very well. We should reach the Azores some time next week.

July 2, 1944

Everything is still going along smooth. The boys are getting a little restless. That's because of such a long ride and doing the same thing over and over. We had a nice chicken dinner this afternoon. And most of the crew are on watch and the rest are sleeping.

July 3, 1944

This is a very bad looking morning. The water is very still and the fog is low. It is also raining. An ideal morning for an attack from a sub. Later on this afternoon while sleeping I was awakened by the general alarm signal. I jumped in my clothes and ran to the signal bridge. The captain then said that one of the other ships had contacted a sub and was making a run on it. Evidently, the sub must have gotten away and we didn't have any trouble during the night.

July 4, 1944

Today is the 4th of July and all we can see is water. I think that everyone aboard ship is a little home sick today. But there's a war going on. A few guns were fired and also one shower signal [a shell that burst illuminating the area under it]. It reminded you a little of celebrating the fourth but in a military manner. We had a very nice dinner and a movie afterwards.

The First Crossing of the Atlantic

July 5, 1944

All is quiet and most of the crew are asleep. The boys have painted the deck and bulkheads. The weather is fair and cooler and partly cloudy. Nothing out of the ordinary happened today. This is our second week at sea since leaving the last port.

July 6, 1944

The sea is a little rough this morning and the sun is coming up from the east. We have sighted land. It is the Pico Mts [on one of the Azores] which is about 7,613 ft. high and it is very pretty. It is hard to believe your own eyes. You can see it for a distance of 75 miles and a volcano is at the peak of the mountain. It is a wonderful sight to see.

July 7, 1944

We arrived in the Azores yesterday evening—on the island of Horta. I've never seen anything as beautiful as this place. It is far prettier than Bermuda. The Azores are neutral but there is an Italian sub there. We can't go ashore, because there are so many spies there and we never know at what time something may happen and we would have to leave in a hurry. This island has an abundant amount of fruit, tobacco, cereal, cattle, wine, and coffee. But I guess that we will be leaving for England in a few days. Even the captain could not go ashore.

July 8, 1944

Here we are anchored in Port Horta in the Azores and it is just like a painting of some kind. The island is composed mostly of Portuguese people. We are not allowed any liberty as yet, because they have some drink which was supposed to have killed one of the British sailors on a merchant ship. The name of this drink is aquardiente [literally "fire water"]. I don't know what is going to be done about it. There has never been an American sailor on liberty on this island. Everyone aboard ship is very angry about not having liberty. You can't even buy souvenirs. But this is a wonderful place to see.

> [Throughout their service, crew members hoped to obtain souvenirs wherever they went. As Dunn explains, souvenirs were a way "to remember what we were doing. . . . You bring them home and keep them, a keepsake."
>
> While none of the *Mason*'s crew were granted shore leave on this occasion, some were given shore duties. The ship's War Diary for July 8 recorded that men were "assigned shore patrol duties for the purpose of rounding up merchant seamen who had gotten ashore in bum boats," small craft bringing provisions out to the merchant ships in the convoy {World War II War Diary Collection, Naval Historical Center, Washington Naval Yard, Washington, D.C.}.]

July 9, 1944

This is a beautiful morning and I know all of the boys would like to be home as well as myself. There isn't anything for us to do but stand our guard and sleep. We still can't go ashore on liberty and it looks as though we are not going. We saw a movie tonight and it did help a little.

July 10, 1944

We are still anchored here in this port and the boys are getting very irritable even myself. We are afraid to say anything to them, because you would probably get a good cussing out. I have seen movies of things like this but I never thought that I would experience it. It is very cloudy and the sky and water have met. The peak of the mt. cannot be seen. It seems as though the sea is angry about something this morning, because she is tossing us all about. I think that she expresses her feelings that way. Although the beautiful vineyards on the mountain side need a little water themselves. What a day.

July 12, 1944

Well, we pulled out of the Azores Tuesday evening about four o'clock and all of the crew including the officers could have shouted, since all of us were tired of staying there. We are headed for another unknown destination. But we are going towards England. We have been out for quite some time without any liberty and you know how the boys are feeling. But otherwise the crew is alright.

July 13, 1944

This is a beautiful morning and air smells very good. Most of us are doing our same duties aboard ship and there is no excitement as yet. We are about 700 miles off the coast of France and the Germans have quite a few submarine bases there. And we are 2000 miles from N.Y. The waters are getting more dangerous as we go along. We had anti-aircraft gun practice this afternoon and the Captain was very much pleased with the shooting of the boys. Now another day's work has been done.

July 14, 1944

It is cloudy this morning and the weather looks threatening. We are hoping that we don't run into a storm, because we are making good time. We should reach our destination in seven or eight days if we don't have any trouble. Our food is getting very low and I don't know how we are going to make it back to the states after reaching our destination. Things wouldn't be so hard if we could only receive some mail.

Crew members man one of the USS *Mason's* "pom-pom" antiaircraft guns. Courtesy of James Graham.

July 15, 1944

Things seem to be turning out alright so far as the food is concerned. But I don't know what we are going to do next week. It is still very cloudy today and it looks as though it might be a storm. We were told to secure everything and prepare for a storm. The old Atlantic is acting up today. It seems as though something has made her angry and she is tossing the ship around very badly. She calms down for a while and then starts all over. We contacted something today and thought it to be a sub. All hands were called to their battle stations. All of us on the signal bridge had rifles. But after waiting a while we found out that was only a whale. We have to be more cautious now because we are in range of Nazi planes. If we do, I think that we can keep them busy for awhile.

> [The Allied invasion of Europe, while underway by this time, had not advanced far enough to deprive Germany of air bases on the French coast. Consequently, the Luftwaffe still sent some patrol planes out looking for convoys. The *Mason's* War Diary for July 18 observed that

an "unidentified plane . . . passed overhead . . . maneuvered around . . . plane last seen heading for St. Nazaire, France, apparently a 'snooper.'"]

July 16, 1944

The Atlantic is still raging and the winds are really howling. It makes you think of a movie you might have seen. We know that we are going to England but don't know what place in England. We will know in about seven more days. You can really appreciate the good old U.S.A. We had chow this evening and it was very slim. And you could not eat it in comfort, because the ship was tossing too much. You could hardly stand up. The storm finally ceased and things were very quiet during the night.

[Storms were a fact of life for convoys crossing the North Atlantic. Dunn remembers that the North Atlantic was "too rough, the toughest thing I ever saw . . . the Atlantic Ocean will eat you up."]

July 17, 1944

We were awakened at 0455 this morning and had general quarters at 0510 but we secured about 0535. After washing up I went on watch with Tubby [William Jones] who is a friend of mine on the signal bridge. He sent one message at 0620. And around about 0730 an airplane approached the convoy from the north. We immediately tried to identify it, which we did in a few minutes. We found it to be a British plane which must have come from an aircraft carrier, because a plane of its type which was the Swordfish usually operates from carriers. One of our officers a little later sights an object in the water dead ahead of us and said that it was a submarine. But after close observation we find it to be a huge whale. As I mentioned once before that we really know our work but the officers don't like to be caught making an error and therefore we are wrong when we are right.

21

CHAPTER 1

July 18, 1944

Well, we are still a good way from our destination and the crew are all edges. It is a very nice day. But the wind is very strong. The general alarm sounded this evening and everyone manned their stations but as usual it was a false alarm. Just as everyone was securing from general quarters another alarm was sounded but it was a false alarm. We were up until midnight before the secure signal was sounded.

July 19, 1944

Just about dawn this morning a plane flew over the ship but we could not identify it. The signal force is very busy these days and all of us have to be very careful, because if we are challenged by another ship of the allied forces and do not answer correctly, they will fire on us at once. We didn't have any general quarters at all tonight and the boys got a good night's sleep.

July 20, 1944

It is a very bad morning and the rain is really coming down. We should reach our destination by Saturday. The convoy is supposed to split up and each destroyer escort will take several ships in different directions. We have been catching plenty of hell on the signal bridge today receiving and sending radio messages. The rain would beat you in the face and it was very hard reading the lights from other ships. But we finally got everything under control.

July 21, 1944

We have been traveling through a storm all day and it really has been tough going. We entered St. George channel tonight and ran into another convoy headed back to the states with British destroyers. Finally we saw lights along the coast and it was land once more. It was good for sore eyes. But we kept going ahead.

> [During the storm, the *Mason's* War Diary of July 21 observed, the "entire mast and rigging {were} enveloped in St. Elmo's Fire. All radios faded out completely."]

July 22, 1944

We are heading straight up the channel and we can see land very good. But still don't know where we are going. Five of the ships in the convoy left us with one of our DEs for another port. The temperature has changed considerably since we have entered this channel. Late this evening two more of our DEs left us to scout and that only leaves two of us with the rest of the convoy.

July 23, 1944

It is a nice morning but a little cloudy. The water is very calm and the sea gulls are following the ship for food. They don't know that we might have to eat some of them for a meal or two. We have sighted small towns all along the coast and they look very peaceful. The rumor is that we are going to Glasgow, Scotland and should get there on Tuesday. We are between Ireland and England. Six more of the ships in the convoy left us and there are only seven left to be delivered. After they reach their destination we will proceed to the London area. We ran into another convoy going the opposite direction and it had two destroyers, one submarine and an aircraft carrier escorting them.

July 24, 1944

Early this morning we finished delivering the rest of the convoy and proceeded to a port close by. We arrived in Belfast, Ireland, about seven thirty this morning and it is really a beautiful seaport town. I've often read of towns like these but this is my first time of ever seeing it. It looks like something you see in movies. I don't know if we will get liberty here or not but all of us sure need it. We have been out to sea for forty-four days without seeing a person or land. We would like to pick up some souvenirs if possible. They finally granted the second section of our crew liberty this afternoon from one o'clock until eight Tuesday morning and the boys really deserve every bit of it and more. I think the ship is getting worse all of the time, because some of the officers try to run their departments and others too. Some of them don't want to give you credit for knowing anything at all. Most of the crew would get off of this if it was possible. Even the officers kick and argue among themselves. I think we are going back to the states from Ireland—at least I hope so. Most of the crew have gone ashore. Our ship pulled up in the City of Belfast and some of the Irishmen came alongside of our ship and talked for quite a while. They wanted American cigarettes and candy. They say that the city is fine. They are very friendly. I know why people come to Europe: because of the beautiful scenery and things are rather cheap. So the night passes away.

July 25, 1944

About five of us went out on liberty today and had a nice time. Everyone treats you very nice. Color doesn't mean a thing to them. In fact they like all of the colored soldiers and sailors far better than the white. Quite a few of the colored soldiers have married girls over here. The white sailors and soldiers from the states have tried to poison the minds of the Irish people against the Negro but they found out that they had lied and now the people won't hardly speak to a white sailor. All of the Colored soldiers have moved into France for the invasion, and the people hated to see them leave. The Negro is treated better anyplace but the United States.

[In later interviews all of the *Mason's* African American crew members commented on how well they had been treated in Belfast. Here they were seen as American fighting men, and they faced no discrimination because of race. In Northern Ireland they were "Yanks," not "Tan Yanks." Dunn says of his love for the people there, "Those people were nice! They were lovely people. You had good liberty there. . . . You hated to leave them." In March 1995 the surviving crew members returned to Belfast for a commemorative visit. See Kelly, *Proudly We Served*, chap. 5.]

2

Hunter-Killer

July 26–September 1, 1944

The USS Mason *usually acted as an escort for convoys crossing the North Atlantic, but she sometimes worked in concert with other warships as a member of hunter-killer groups searching for German submarines. Directed to wolfpacks by British reports—the British had cracked the German naval code and so could often pinpoint a wolfpack's location from intercepted radio transmissions—and by her own Huff-Duff equipment, the* Mason *sought to sink submarines. Such was her duty while returning to America with four other destroyer escorts after her first crossing of the Atlantic. Dunn says that destroyer escorts were especially well suited for hunter-killer work because they "could turn on a dime, just about."*

In one of his newspaper articles about the Mason, *the war correspondent on board, Thomas Young, captured the excitement of this aspect of the ship's work: "Then came one of the greatest thrills of the entire trip, when we learned that our task force, consisting entirely of destroyer escorts, was to return to the United States, without a convoy, as a 'killer group.' This time we were to go off the defensive and take the offensive. . . . We were going out looking for the enemy, to find him and destroy him" (quoted in Kelly,* Proudly We Served, *p. 96).*

After duties with the hunter-killer group, the Mason *engaged in training exercises in Casco Bay, Maine, and then prepared to escort her second convoy to the United Kingdom.*

26

July 26, 1944

We got underway this morning and are on own way back to New York and should arrive there next Tuesday or Wednesday. We are going at top speed and will probably stay that way until we reach the States.

July 27, 1944

We are still rolling on towards the states and the weather is beginning to get much better. All of the crew are anxious to get back to our homeland once more. I think this has been a very nice trip and we have been very lucky. But with the help of God we made it over and now are on our way home.

July 28, 1944

Things seem to be going pretty good for the time being. But it is still raining and the sea is raging. About 2:00 P.M. this afternoon our Commodore contacted two subs and the general alarm was sounded. All of the DEs were ready for action in the North Atlantic. We trailed them for about half an hour and then we all made runs on them and dropped depth charges. They tried to fight back but we were too much for them. We dropped sixty-five cans [depth charges] on them and they did the job. We proceeded on our way.

> [The *Mason's* War Diary for July 28 described the action: "At 1322, all hands at battle stations. STERN {the commodore's ship} appeared to have good sonar contact. All ships maneuvered in box formation five (5) miles from contact point. At 1930, secured from battle stations, and rejoined formation with other ships."]

July 29, 1944

We are still trying to struggle through this rough sea. We are under water just about as much as we are on top. My friend Tubby and myself were drenched this afternoon while on watch. The water came over the bridge. I am having an awful time writing. Half of the crew is seasick and it is too rough to cook so you can see what we are up against. I dread going back on watch tonight. But with the help of the Lord we will make it home safely. We have to wear life jackets to go anyplace on the deck.

July 30, 1944

It is cloudy this morning and the sea is calm. We came through the last storm alright. But later we had engine trouble, but we had it running again in a little while. All of the boys are still watching and waiting to see the good old terra firma (firm land) once more. Late tonight we received a message to proceed into the Boston Harbor instead of New York and that was good news for us to hear. We are all hoping that we will get leave so we can go home to see our loved ones. We should pull into Boston Wednesday, August 2, 1944. So time marches on.

July 31, 1944

It is very foggy this morning and it is drizzling rain and the sea is beginning to get rough again. We are just off the coast of New Foundland and it has been very cold. But the weather is warming up now. The boys are all busy getting their clothes clean, shining their shoes and looking at train schedules. Just a few minutes ago our executive officer announced that we would get four days leave. But the boys thought sure that they would get at least seven. I, like the rest, had the same idea and had planned on going home to visit my mother. But you can never plan anything in the Navy. Because you are here today and gone tomorrow. Nevertheless we will have to take it and be satisfied. We finally pulled into Boston on the 2nd of August and were given four days leave.

[Shore leave was a time to be savored. Dunn explains what he did on leave. "You go home, if you have enough time to go home." There "you could go to the movies, you could go to bars, or to visit somebody you know." For Dunn, home meant Newport, where his wife was working. But on occasion Jane joined him in another city. In New York they would meet at the Mandalay, a favorite bar in Harlem, and Dunn would take the el from the Brooklyn Naval Yard. "We would talk and lollygag," he remembers. Sometimes the wives of the crew members would get together and go shopping, while the men "would take it easy and talk."

After leave ended, the *Mason* went to Casco Bay for training exercises with other ships—a period Dunn only sporadically recorded—in preparation for escorting another convoy to Europe.]

August 15, 1944

We went to Casco Bay which is in Portland, Maine. There we had gun practice every day for one week [in] which we outshot every ship up there.

[The *Mason*'s captain wrote his parents a letter on August 25 with much the same pride that Dunn expressed in this diary entry: "The ship is really coming along in very fine shape except that every time we get in they practically rebuild us with new stuff always coming out {a reference to new sonar and radar equipment}. . . . Compared with other ships of the same type I think we are a little better in most things such as gunnery than the majority of them, and have a smooth working outfit." Dunn's remembrance is similar: "We worked good together, just like a machine, smooth most of the time."]

August 29, 1944

We left Portland Thursday August 24 and arrived in Boston the same day. We stayed there four days. On Monday August 28 we pulled out with three destroyer escorts and two cargo ships. We are

supposed to meet a convoy which is going to Europe. We caught
the convoy this morning about 0530 and it is very large. It has two
aircraft carriers with it. But the exact destination is unknown. The
convoy consists of about fifty ships.

August 30, 1944

We stayed with this huge convoy until about eight o'clock this
morning. Then the Captain of a destroyer came aboard our ship
and we reversed our course. We are taking him back to Casco Bay
in Portland, Maine. We have run into an awful gale and all of us
were ordered to wear life jackets. This baby is really pitching and
rolling. Half of the crew is seasick and can't eat anything. We
should reach Portland tomorrow evening.

August 31, 1944

We had an awful tough time last night. The ship was just about on
her side and it was all we could do to keep from falling out of our
bunks. It calmed down this morning and we are steadily forging
ahead. We fired our guns and depth charges just for practice this
afternoon.

September 1, 1944

We are now starting our sixth month on this battle wagon and it
hasn't been bad at all. We arrived in Portland, Maine this morning
about six o'clock. We put Captain Poole off and didn't waste any
time in getting underway again. He is the captain that we picked
up about 1,000 miles out in the Atlantic Ocean. Our Captain said,
"Next stop New York," and all of us were very happy, because we
thought that we were going to stay in Maine. We will arrive in the
morning sometime. This ship has actually fooled some people, be-

cause the boys can handle their jobs better than they expected. They don't know what to do with us now.

[The *Mason* was hardly a "battle wagon," slang usually reserved for battleships. Dunn's use of the term may have been an indication of the pride he felt in his ship.

After Captain Poole was delivered to his ship in Casco Bay, the *Mason* sailed for New York City to begin escorting a convoy to the United Kingdom.]

3

The Raging Sea: Convoy N.Y. 119

September 19–November 5, 1944

As much as German submarines, the sea was the enemy of convoys. The USS Mason *and her charges felt the full wrath of the North Atlantic while escorting Convoy N.Y. 119 from New York City to Great Britain. Composed mainly of small army tug boats and small oilers intended for work in Europe's coastal waters, the convoy was hit by one of the worst storms of World War II. Making matters worse, the tugs were pulling large, ungainly wooden barges and railroad car floats to be beached and used as temporary docks on the coast of France. These were the makings of a near disaster.*

September 19, 1944

We arrived in New York Sept. 2 and stayed until the 19th. On the morning of the 19th we got underway at 5:42 A.M. We are starting out with a convoy composed of army tugs. They are very slow and it will take us at least forty days or more to cross the Atlantic to our destination which will be France and England. The European War should be over by the time we get back home.

September 20, 1944

We had quite a bit of trouble with some of the ships in the convoy last night. They had either dropped back or gotten away from the rest of the ships. We are traveling southeastward and the weather is

The USS *Mason* at sea. Courtesy of Mansel G. Blackford.

warming up quite a bit. Although it has been raining for about a day and a half, it is fine outside this afternoon. A navy blimp came over head this morning and sent a message saying that she would escort us until dark this evening. The crew as a whole were in a good mood but we were short of men. Most of the boys are taking it easy, except those men on watch. Most of us were kind of glad to get back to sea. It means that we will have a nice bankroll when we get back home.

September 21, 1944

Last night two of the ships were two miles ahead of the convoy and I had to send two messages to them by light. Later one of the same ships showed two vertical red lights indicating a breakdown. But we continued on our regular course. Today we met another convoy coming from Europe. Their destination was New York. Things are just about the same aboard ship and nothing new has happened.

CHAPTER 3

September 22, 1944

Well, here I am again and every time I open my book I look right into the eyes of my little Jane. Just looking at her seems to give me more ambition. The weather is pretty bad out this morning. The rain is really coming down and all of us are below deck. We just sit around telling each other our experiences. And some of them are a mess. A plane flew over us this morning but we identified it before it reached our ship. These boys are really on the ball.

September 23, 1944

It is beautiful out today and all of the ships are steadily forging ahead. Several of the ships have lagged far behind and we had to go back and escort them until they caught up with the rest of the convoy. This has been an easy trip so far for our division. I don't think that we will encounter any submarines, but one never knows, does one?

[The phrase "one never knows, does one?"—a phrase Dunn repeats several times in his diary—may have come from a popular tune of the day by Fats Waller. The line in the song is "One never knows, do one?" As Dunn says, "You pick up things like that."]

September 24, 1944

I was awakened this Sunday morning at four o'clock to go on watch and it was very rough outside. The wind was howling and the raging sea seemed to be very angry. She was tossing us to and fro and from side to side. Water came up on the bridge and I drank quite a bit of salt water. This afternoon turned out to be very pretty but the sea is still acting up. But the Mason forges on toward her destination.

The Raging Sea

September 25, 1944

The sea is still raging this morning and has been that way all night. You couldn't stay in your bunk at all. All of the ships are having a very hard time, especially the small army tugs. One of them sank last night and we are out looking for men on a life raft. Also a boy fell over the side of one of the destroyer escorts and hasn't been found yet. I am this moment bracing myself to write this in my book. People shouldn't condemn a sailor so much for what he does while in port, because you don't know the hell he goes thru at sea. Well, it has calmed down quite a bit and the sun is out. I had my evening chow and went to sleep.

September 26, 1944

I came on watch at midnight and it was very cloudy and the sea had gotten rough again. It started to rain and we were in for another tough night. Around one thirty one of the tugs sent out an S.O.S. that she was sinking. Four of the DEs went to her rescue. It had 13 men aboard and 12 had abandoned ship while one of them had gotten trapped below and couldn't get out. Searchlights were all over the water. It looked like New York harbor. Ten of the men were accounted for, while the others were lost at sea. We searched all morning but couldn't find any of them. It was very pathetic and yet sailors catch hell when they come back to the states. It is still raining and the water is rough. We will probably lose some more tonight.

September 27, 1944

Things went along smoothly last night. We didn't have any more trouble at all. It is very pretty out this morning and the convoy is going along fine, although I am sorry that those men lost their lives the night before last. We found the rest of the ships yesterday and they were very glad to see us. I was just looking at Jane's picture this morning and I miss her and my mother an awful lot. I love the two of them very much and that means until death do us part. I guess most of the boys feel the same way about their families or girl friends. When you love someone that you know you can depend on, it really helps you to carry out your job. Love is a great thing. This afternoon one of the army tugs needed some spare parts for her engines and we had to get them to her some way or the other. We pulled beside of it and shot a line across to the tug with our gun. On this end was a rubber boat which one of our men was in. Our boys and the boys on the tug worked nicely to get the rubber boat across to the tug and the boy handed things out of the boat to the fellows on the tug and then proceeded back. It was a thrilling event for the boy. Pictures were taken of him by an army cameraman. So you see the army and the navy are still working together.

September 28, 1944

All is quiet and we are taking it easy today. Nothing of any importance has happened and the ships are making a fairly good speed. I have been reading "Strange Fruits" all day and finally finished it. We had general quarters this afternoon and fired our guns several times then secured and had our evening chow. I am going on watch at eight o'clock tonite. I am also trying to study for my examination for an advancement in rating by November 1st.

> [*Strange Fruit* was a controversial novel about lynching by Lillian Smith, a southern white woman. A later song by Billie Holiday summarized the book's point with the famous line "Southern trees bear strange fruit." The *Mason* had, Dunn relates, "a little library with books for you to read and keep yourself occupied." It is unlikely that the library possessed as controversial a book as *Strange Fruit*, however. Most likely Dunn brought the book on board himself or borrowed it from a crewmate.]

Seamen advanced in ratings by passing examinations given by officers. Seamen emerged from their initial naval training as seamen-strikers
(as apprentices), from which they advanced to seaman third class, seaman second class, seaman first class, and chief (third class). Dunn says
that the men helped each other try to advance in their ratings. "We
taught each other. . . . We would help each other." Some officers, he remembers, were better than others in helping the men advance.

Dunn wrote the following and similar diary entries as if they were
letters to his wife.]

Dear Jane,

I have been thinking about you very much and I just had to
write you. Daily I miss you terribly and I dream of you at all times.
For some reason I worry about you very much, because I know you
were not feeling well when I left you. Nevertheless I hope that you
are much better. I am feeling pretty good but my heart yearns for
you and mother. You'll never have to worry about me leaving you
nor going with some other woman, because as I told you before
the navy makes you think of the past or gives you plenty of time to
think things over. You have been a good wife and have lived up to
your bargain. I have all the faith in the world in you and I hope that
I can always say that. We are going to be very happy after all of this
is over. I know my love for you shall never die. The boys talk about
what a wonderful wife I have and I am very proud of you. Take care
of yourself and be a good girl. Your Hubby.

September 29, 1944

It is a fairly nice day and the sun is trying to come out. The convoy
seems to be moving pretty good, but now and then some of the
ships fall back. We refueled at sea today and it is very interesting to
watch. It took us about three hours to refuel. All of the white boys
came out and looked at our ship. I guess it was the first of ever seeing an all colored ship. I fell coming out of the chow hall this

evening and pulled a muscle in my side and it is giving me a little trouble but you can't hurt an old sea wolf like myself.

September 30, 1944

Well, we have 18 more days to go before reaching our destination and I can take them standing on my head as long as I know that my little Jane is waiting to see me when I return. It is very beautiful to-day and the ships are moving steadily thru the ink blue water and the sun is beaming down on them. All of us have been sitting around talking this afternoon. Just something to occupy our minds. It really helps at times. We have a lot of time to think about what we are going to do after this war is over. After the war in Europe is over I think that we will be shifted to the South Pacific and that is bad. And so ends another day. The sun is going down and it looks as though it is setting right on the water. It resembles a large yellow orange.

[Concern about going to the Pacific would mount, especially as the war wound down in Europe in the spring of 1945. As Dunn explains, "We did not want to go. . . . We just did not want to cross the line. . . . Enough was enough."]

October 1, 1944

It is fairly nice this morning and the sun is shining. The convoy has speeded up a little and that makes things a little better. I slept most of the morning. Things are usually quiet on Sundays. A Bible class was held aboard ship this afternoon and it seems to be alright. Nothing of any importance has happened, so ends another day.

October 2, 1944

I was up at 4:00 A.M. this morning to go on watch and the moon was still up and very pretty. The weather is nice and warm and the sun has come up above the water on the horizon. What a sight.

Most of the boys are studying for their rates which I am doing myself. The morning passed very fast and we are having noon chow. Afterwards I took one of my examinations and passed. If I do make my second class I will probably be transferred to the South Pacific. The convoy is still progressing very nicely. When we get to our destination we will have travelled 3,800 miles. I have just had my bath and I guess that I will call it a night, because I have a watch at 4:00 o'clock in the morning. Sweet dreams, my darling wife Jane.

October 3, 1994

"Ah," what a beautiful morning. The sun is coming up and the air smells very good. The deck forces are washing down the deck and the other boys are just lounging about the deck and sleeping. I did some sewing this morning and finished about noon. About two o'clock we had firing practice for an hour. Then around five o'clock we contacted a submarine and [the] alarm was sounded. Everyone rushed to their battle stations. We passed right over it but didn't drop any depth charges. The ship behind us dropped five but the sub maneuvered out of the way. We searched for it about two hours and didn't pick it up anymore. We figured that it must have gone under the convoy and you can't pick it up with our sound gear, because we wouldn't know whether it was their engines or the ships in the convoy that we hear. So we will call it a day and wish for better luck next time. We'll get one yet.

October 4, 1944

Well, it's just about the same old story. Nothing exciting, nothing new. We have run into a gale and it has blown us off of our regular course. I hardly know what is going on above deck unless I am going on watch because I am sleeping or doing something or the other below most of the time. When it is about six o'clock in the evening, we darken ship and turn in.

Mary Jane Dunn, 1943. Courtesy of James A. Dunn.

October 5, 1944

Dear Jane,

Here I am again and I really miss you very much. Sometimes I just sit and think of the good times we have had together. I have been thinking about what I would do after the war. I have had several ideas but I'll wait and consult you before doing anything about it. I want you to be happy and enjoy this like one should. You know I had a dream last night and it was a very good one. It seemed so real I almost had to change my sheet. The ship rolled and I was awakened. But it was good. Well, I feel better now that I have written you a few lines. Be sweet. I shall always love you. Your devoted hubby, James A. Dunn.

October 6, 1945

Well, we are still forging ahead but not very fast. The convoy is only doing five knots at the most and sometimes three. So you can see what a tiresome trip this is. We are still standing watches and sleeping. I have heard all of the World Series games so far and enjoy them very much. Some of the boys are betting on the Series. We will pass through the Azores in the morning some time or other, but we are not going to stop this time. After reaching our destination, I hope that we will return to the states immediately.

October 7, 1944

Today we reached the Azores and we are now passing one of the islands known as the Flores. It is the largest of the five islands here. The population is not very large. All of the boys are watching the beautiful island wishing that they could set foot on land for just a short while. But we are not stopping this time until we reach our destination which should be about fourteen more days. I have been reading a book all day called "The Spirit of the Border," by Zane Grey and it is really very interesting.

October 8, 1944

It is a beautiful Sunday morning with the sun coming up from the east and the sea is very calm and blue. All of that said, we would like to be home on such a pretty morning. In sight now is the highest mountain that I have ever seen. It is Mt. Pico. I mentioned it once before. It joins the island of Fayal which is a smaller island than the rest but is very picturesque. The peak of the mountain is covered with white rolls of clouds and the ink-blue water breaks at the bottom of it.

Dear Jane,

I really wish that you could see these islands and this mountain. But, honey, my greatest ambition is to get back safely to see you

41

and mother. The admiral tried to act up a little last night. He knew that I was thinking of you and tried to take advantage of me but I made an agreement with him. I agreed to see that he would be well taken care of when we get back home and he seemed to be satisfied. De Cuir [Manuel De Cuir], Johny and another boy and myself play pinochle every now and then to pass the time. We are headed into France and I imagine that it is all torn up from bombs being dropped over there. Well, my dear, take care and be a good girl. I love you more and more every day. Forever Yours, James Dunn.

[Like most middle-class Americans, white and black, of his time, Dunn dissembled a bit about his sexual feelings, hence his use of the term "admiral" here and throughout his diary. As an African American male, he may have also been keeping his sex life private so as not to feed racist stereotypes about "oversexed" blacks.]

October 9, 1944

The crew was awakened at 5:00 A.M. this morning so we would be ready to refuel our ship at eight o'clock. We pulled up beside the tanker and refueled in about an hour and then took our position in the convoy. While refueling, our communications officer asked an officer on the other ship if he had received all of a message regarding our route to England and our destination, since our boys had missed some of it over the radio. So the officer had one of his signalmen send it to us. We received every bit of it and found out that we are going to Falmouth, England on the southern end of the English Channel just across from France. A little French town that the Americans have just taken. We will probably reach our destination on the 20th of October. I attended Bible class yesterday and it was very nice. An American plane flew over us and we identified it immediately as the B-25 Mitchell. And so another day passes by.

October 10, 1944

The weather is much different today. It has gotten colder and the sea is very rough. We have run into another gale and it's really rough. We will be very lucky if we can make it without losing any more of the ships out of the convoy. I have been feeling bad the last day or two. It is mostly a cold in my chest. Together we fight. Together we stand, until we reach our homeland.

October 11, 1944

It is still very rough today. We tossed all night with water covering all of the top decks. You have to be very careful walking along the decks, because a large wave might wash you over the side. After taking some medicine last night, I feel a lot better today. We have been playing pinochle all day to pass away the time.

October 12, 1944

We are still trying to get thru this storm without losing any more tugs. The sea is still raging and some of the swells are as high as the ship. They look like mountains. The wind has blown us off of our course and we are trying very hard to get back on it. Everything is just about the same. So I will hit my sack until midnight when I go on duty.

> [The *Mason's* War Diary for October 12 recorded "convoy having great difficulty in maintaining proper formation. Convoy averaging 15 degrees leeway {that is, winds and waves were pushing it 15 degrees off course}. It will be impossible to pass through routed positions at this rate."]

October 13, 1944

Well, this is supposed to be the day of [unclear]. I went on duty today at noon and it is still very bad out. It is getting foggy and the wind and rain are beating against me very hard. Some of the ships are just about lost. About 2:00 P.M. I received a message from one of the tugs towing two barges. It said, "Need assistance immedi-

43

ately; our barges are sinking." I reported the message to the officer of the deck and he notified the Commodore [of the convoy] at once. Both of us went to the rescue. The Commodore, seeing that he could not save the barges, decided to sink them by gunfire. They shot their large guns at the barge but failed to get any results. They were not hitting it. So he told me that he had heard about our good shooting. To go ahead and try our luck. So we began to fire and in about fifteen or twenty minutes we had sunk the barge. We only missed two out of twelve shots. So the Mason is still living up to old traditions.

October 14, 1944

Well, everything is under control once more, but the weather is still bad. I slept all morning and went on duty at noon. An American plane flew over our convoy and I answered her challenge very quickly. We should reach our destination about Tuesday or Wednesday. The Commodore of our Task Group sent us a message this afternoon, congratulating the Mason's gun crew on their good shooting yesterday. And he also stated that we had one of the finest crews that he has seen. Our Captain had a smile all over his face. He was very pleased with the boys. I heard the entire Ohio State and Wisconsin football game this evening and enjoyed it very much, in which Ohio State won by a score of 20-7. And now I am climbing into my sack. I have a midnite watch and lights are now going out.

> [The message from the commodore read, "Due to the stress and strain of events yesterday I may have forgotten to give you and your excellent gunners a well-deserved 'well done' for their effective shooting. The Mason has performed each task assigned in a most commendable manner. Please convey my appreciation to your excellent crew" {14 October 1944, copy in the editor's possession}.]

Firing one of the 3″ guns, Roger Rorie (left) and Leonard Coleman (right). Courtesy of James Graham.

October 15, 1944

It is another beautiful Sunday morning at sea and everyone seems to be in a good mood. The convoy is moving a little faster and that is good news to our ears. After having noon chow I went on watch and it began to rain about two o'clock. DuFau and myself talked of what we would be doing if we were home with our wives on a Sunday like this and the four hours went by so fast I hardly realized it. Bible class was held again this afternoon but I was on watch and could not make it. Everything has been very quiet today and the crew is sitting around writing letters, which they might beat home, and the others were listening to the radio broadcast from New York City and England.

October 16, 1944

This morning found us a little closer to our destination. The sea is still raging and pitching our ship from side to side. All of the ships of the convoy are scattered about and we are trying to round them up just like a shepherd rounding up his sheep. The North Atlantic really lives up to its name. The rough Atlantic. Late this afternoon a call came over the P.A. system for all signalmen to report to the signal bridge, and all of us were there in nothing flat. We were changing course and the message had to be sent to every tug in the convoy. We were waiting for something like this anyway. And the four of us sure did lay it on them. It was fast and short. It is now 6:45 P.M. and I am listening to Amos and Andy [a popular radio program]. However it is only 2:45 P.M. in the states. So I am signing off until tomorrow.

> [By this date, as noted in the *Mason*'s War Diary of October 16, the wind had risen to forty knots: "Wind and seas rising. Many breakdowns reported by small craft and increasing difficulty with tow wires."]

October 17, 1944

Our ship has taken seventeen small oilers and gone ahead of the rest of the convoy. It is still very rough and we have to be awful careful. We stayed busy all morning sending messages. The chow is getting bad and they don't have anything but beef and potatoes left. I only eat soup. We are not far from England and we should see the beacon light at midnight. The sea is alright for a single man. But the married man should be home with his wife.

[On October 16 the commodore of the convoy divided the convoy into several groups. He sent the *Mason* ahead with fourteen small oilers, four tug boats, and several other ships.]

October 18, 1944

We sighted the beacon light last night and are now heading up the English Channel. We have a lot of responsibility taking all of these boats into Falmouth, England. They are hard to keep together because of the sea being so rough. We sighted the coast of England about 11:30 A.M. and it really looks good after being out here one month today without stopping. The rest of the convoy is about forty miles behind us. They ran into a storm last night and lost one ship and seven men. We might have to go back after them.

[According to the *Mason's* War Diary of October 18, winds "reached a maximum of 70–80 knots" with "visibility zero." These were hurricane-strength winds.]

October 19, 1944

We took our group of ships into England yesterday evening safe and sound. Two British ships met us in the Channel to help us the rest of the way. The weather is still very bad and a terrific storm is coming up. Around about six o'clock we received word from the Commodore to come back out to sea to help escort the other ships in. The two British ships started back with us but later turned back because the sea was too rough. But we had to keep going. It didn't look as though we were going to make it but with the help of the Lord we made it safely. We have never been in a storm as rough as that one. It has calmed down a little now and we are searching for lost ships and survivors. We should reach Plymouth, England this evening or in the morning. We have decided not to go back until

we find some of the other ships. We sighted three of the army tugs
and gave them their directions to Falmouth England. We also got a
dispatch from one of our DEs that they were down to bread and
water. They are trying to make it into Plymouth, England. But we
have orders to keep searching for some of the barges that came
over with us. Well, it is now nine o'clock and I am turning in. At
ten thirty we got a contact with a submarine and the general alarm
was sounded. Everyone went out of their sacks in record time,
some with clothes on and some without. We waited and waited but
nothing has happened so far [unclear]. Several boys were hurt during the mixup.

> [Alfred L. Lind, the commodore of convoy N.Y. 119, reported in his
> report on the convoy that by October 18 seas were running thirty to
> fifty feet. Nonetheless, the *Mason* delivered her section of the convoy
> safely to Falmouth, England. Lind noted that "no doubt many of
> these small craft and the lives of the men on them were saved due to
> the untiring efforts and good seamanship displayed by the . . . *Mason*."
> In getting her part of the convoy into harbor, the *Mason* was dam-
> aged; she had had her radio antennae blown away and had suffered
> further damage "to the extent of having several welded seams open in
> her decks and two longitudinal strength members . . . adrift." After
> emergency repairs, the "plucky" *Mason,* now assisted by two British
> sloops, turned back "and began plowing into 40 foot seas" to help
> bring in more ships from the convoy. The commodore observed that
> "shortly after they emerged from the channel . . . both British Sloops
> refused to proceed further and returned to anchorage." The *Mason*
> persisted in rejoining the convoy and helped bring in the rest of the
> ships. In his report Commodore Lind wrote that he "considers the
> performance of the USS *Mason,* her Commanding Officer, Officers,
> and men outstanding and recommends that this ship be given a letter
> of commendation to be filed in the record of each officer and man on
> board that vessel" {"U.S. Atlantic Fleet, Task Group 27.5," 8 October
> 1944, Serial 002, World War II Action Report, Escort Division 80,
> Naval Historical Center, Washington Navy Yard, Washington D.C.}.

But for fifty years nothing happened. The commodore's report was lost in the navy's records. After my father died in 1988, and my mother in 1992, I found a copy of the commodore's report in my father's personal papers. When Mary Pat Kelly contacted me in 1993 while she was researching her book, I sent the copy to her. She then found the original in the navy archives, and she was able to use the report to win recognition for the men of the *Mason*. They were all awarded letters of commendation by the secretary of the navy at a special ceremony in Washington, D.C., on February 16, 1995.

For more detail on the convoy as a whole, see Charles Dana Gibson, *The Ordeal of Convoy N.Y. 119* (New York: South Seaport Museum, 1973).]

October 20, 1944

The boys have to be very careful walking above on deck. The water is coming over it. We were told to wear life jackets. We received word from the Commodore stating that a hurricane was coming in behind us and to try and get in before night falls. We are about two hundred and fifty miles out. We have our engines as high as they will go and it looks as if we might make it at six o'clock this evening. Well, we are still in the Channel and it looks as though we will arrive in Plymouth behind schedule. We beat the storm in and are now passing Falmouth, England. It is pitch dark. Everyone is very tired and worn out and a couple of days rest will do us all good. We pulled into Plymouth at 12:35 P.M. and dropped anchor.

October 21, 1944

This morning we got underway to refuel from a tanker in the harbor. This seems to be a nice little town. But the German air force have bombed it quite a bit. Over half the people have evacuated this town. They have girls working on the smaller boats. We are about four hours ride by train from London England. But I know

THE SECRETARY OF THE NAVY
WASHINGTON, D.C. 20350-1000

The Secretary of the Navy takes pleasure in commending

USS MASON (DE 529)

for service as set forth in the following

CITATION:

For meritorious service from 18 October 1944 to 19 October 1944 while serving as a member of Task Group 27.5 conducting convoy escort operations in the Atlantic Ocean. On 17 October 1944, USS MASON (DE 529) was placed in charge of an advance group of Convoy NY119. With winds gusting to 70 knots and seas ranging from 30 to 50 feet, MASON safely brought her charges consisting of 14 Y-oilers, 4 ST tugs, and 2 British escort vessels into port at Falmouth, England. The heavy weather opened welded seams in the deck and damaged two longitudinal strength members. Through perseverance so typical of MASON's crew, emergency repairs were effected and MASON proceeded back to the main body of the convoy to assist in recovering lost tows and rounding up the scattered convoy. By their unrelenting determination and steadfast devotion to duty, the officers and crew of USS MASON (DE 529) reflected credit upon themselves and upheld the highest traditions of the United States Naval Service.

John H. Dalton
Secretary of the Navy

Copy of the letter of commendation from the secretary of the navy to the crew of the USS *Mason*.

that we want to get a chance to go there. We lost twenty men out of the convoy coming across.

October 22, 1944

It is a beautiful Sunday morning and we are sitting here in Plymouth, England. Some of the boys were given liberty this morning. Grant [Melvin J. Grant] and Harris went to London over the weekend. It is not far from Plymouth. The rest of us just laid around doing nothing.

October 23, 1944

It is raining this morning and it is a little cool. Some of the boys said that liberty wasn't any good. They said that the white soldiers and sailors are the reason for this. We went on liberty at 1:00 P.M. today and we didn't know where to turn or go. This place has been torn up by the German planes who bombed it very much. We just about walked ourselves to death. The bars didn't open until late this evening and we did manage to get some gin and brandy. Later we went to a small place where they were having a dance. But there wasn't anything much here. Souvenirs couldn't be found any place. So we finally came back to the ship.

[Nonetheless, leave was a welcome relief from the horrors of Convoy N.Y. 119. Dunn does recall that "we relaxed a little bit after we got into Plymouth."]

October 24, 1944

We pulled out this morning to patrol the coast of the English Channel. Nothing of any importance has happened. We are just cruising along and this Channel is rough today. I guess that we will be over here for awhile.

October 25, 1944

Well, we are still patrolling outside of the Channel. Every now and then we run into some kind of contact but it doesn't amount to anything. We are around the British mine field and it is very dangerous. Late in the evening we sighted a large box which looked like a drifting mine. We were ordered to fire on it which we did. But found out it was just a wooden box. Everything seems to quiet down for the day.

October 26, 1944

I had gotten off watch at midnight Wednesday and had been asleep for a short while when the alarm was given around about 1:30 this morning. We had contacted a ship and we knew just how fast it was traveling. You couldn't see your hand before you. We'd followed it for an hour and then overtaken it. We sent a challenge by flashing light and the ship didn't answer. Then we were ordered to fire star shells so we could see the ship as they bursted. The shells went off just above the ship and we could see that it was a merchant vessel. We were getting ready to open fire on it with our big guns when it finally answered. A few more minutes longer and it would have been blown apart. It was a British ship coming from Gibraltar. We finally secured and had a good night's rest.

October 27, 1944

We reached port this morning and anchored. Everything is very quiet and the town seems to be deserted. All of us are just about worn out. There isn't anything to do on liberty. Because everything is closed or has been bombed. We are just hoping that we will leave soon.

October 28, 1944

The boys are not pleased at all with this place but there isn't anything they can do about it. They paid us off again today in English money but I didn't draw any of mine. Because my wife and mother have to have a Xmas present. We are just sitting in port waiting for our convoy to form. We are taking it back to the states. I played a little poker with the boys and won enough to keep me in toilet articles and cigarettes. I miss my wife and mother very much. Of course, I guess all of the boys feel the same way about their loved ones. They showed us a movie tonight and that did ease the tension a little. The lights are going out.

October 29, 1944

Nothing of any importance is happening. Most of the boys are taking it easy. The ship is beginning to get worse. Some of the officers love to put you on report. Some of them haven't been used to handling men. They are slowly breaking down the morale of the men. They still don't mean you any good.

[By officers Dunn meant chief petty officers. There was friction on board between some of the white chief petty officers and the crew, and some of the petty officers would later be transferred off the *Mason*.]

October 30, 1944

We are busy having an inspection this morning. Four boys and myself decide to visit London. After waiting all day we get our papers signed and leave the ship about three o'clock this evening. We took the train out of Plymouth and at four o'clock and it was a thrilling ride. We arrived in London about eleven o'clock that night. Every-

James A. Dunn, photographed while on leave in London in 1944. Courtesy of James A. Dunn.

thing is still blacked out but the people still go about just as though nothing is going on. We found the Red Cross and got a room for the night.

October 31, 1944

We were up this morning at nine o'clock and had breakfast. At ten o'clock we started a tour of the city. The first stop was Charles Dickens Gift shop on Portsmouth St. It was established in 1567 and is four hundred years old. We passed all of the law courts of England, the Lord Mayor of England who is next to the King. In case of the death of the King, the Lord Mayor takes over until a new

54

King is crowned. We crossed the river of Thames over London Bridge. It opens up to let ships pass. We passed the Great Tower of London where all of the great Kings and Queens reigned. It is 1200 yrs. old and several bombs have hit but she is still standing. We visited St. Paul's Cathedral and it is very beautiful inside. It is the largest in the world. We went into the tower where the whispering gallery is located and then to the top of the tower which consists of 627 steps. From this point you can see the City of London. It took them 35 yrs. to build it. From there we proceeded to Westminster Abbey. On our way we passed the House of Parliament, Big Ben, Scotland Yard on Downing St., St. James Palace, Buckingham Palace, Queen Victoria Memorial and the statue of Richard the Lion Hearted. We saw many famous poets in Westminster Abbey. Also the great Clive of India, Shakespeare and Kipling. We also saw the Great Coronation Chamber and behind it buried great Kings and Queens. The unknown soldier is buried here. The statue of Wilberforce from whom the Negro College [in Ohio] was named. This place is over a thousand years old and it is the private property of the King. We saw the statue of Lord Nelson who has one eye and arm. Hyde Park is a very beautiful place. I would have loved for my wife to see these sights. It is something you shall never forget. Several bombs fell tonight, killing a few people.

> [Dunn was so impressed with London that he used Red Cross facilities to telephone his wife, as he recalls, about "how pretty it was" and to tell her about "the castles and churches, Westminster, that I had read about in English history."]

November 1, 1944

Today we took a long stroll down some of the streets. Looking at different places that had been bombed. We all had several pictures made on Oxford St. We didn't have time for anything else. So we caught the 4:15 train this evening and arrived in Plymouth at 11:40 tonight. We all enjoyed the trip and sights very much.

November 2, 1944

Everything is a little quiet and dull aboard ship today. I am just about fed up with this ship, because some of the officers try to take advantage of their rank and superiority. I hope that I don't blow my top before getting back to the states. They don't give you credit for anything. But these boys are no fools. Davis helps them with their dirty work. He loves to stooge for them. I am going to let him have it if he gets smart with me. It's the same old story about Negroes but it is going to be different this time.

November 3, 1944

We are getting ready for another inspection this morning by the Captain. They are treating us just like a bunch of boots just entering the Navy. They forget that some of us are men.

November 4 & 5, 1944

It is the same old thing. Just laying around in the harbor waiting for our sailing orders.

4

Returning to America

November 6–November 22, 1944

The Mason's *crew soon found itself leaving England to escort a convoy of large tugboats back to Norfolk and New York City. Tensions mounted as the men were crowded together on their small ship, and they devised pastimes to while away the hours and relieve the pressure. Dunn says that "we would read, play cards." They watched movies "in the chow hole." Almost anything was tried to get a break from the monotony. Even so there were times, he remembers, when "we didn't know whether to shit or go blind."*

November 6, 1944

We got orders to take a small convoy of large tugs back to the states, and all of us are glad to go home once more. We pulled out this morning at 0715 and saw a transport loaded with colored British subjects. They are getting ready for another invasion. Well, we are homeward bound and I am trying to make two small table lamps for my wife. This should keep me busy during the entire trip.

[The crew members would make lamps using brass three-inch shell casings for their bases—souvenirs of their service.]

November 7, 1944

The sea is very rough today and it is raining. But we don't seem to mind it, because we are going home. We are bringing eleven tugs back to the states. Half of the crew are seasick. I have my lamps just about finished and they look pretty good for an amateur. We are wondering how the election [the 1944 presidential election] is coming along. Grant, our Yeoman, is too lazy to make a lamp for himself and wants Denson [Fred Denson] to make it for him. Most of the boys are making something. Nothing exciting has happened so to bed I go.

November 8, 1944

The storm is still raging this morning and the ship is rolling quite a bit. We heard that Roosevelt won the election as most of us thought he would. It is all we can do to hold our trays in the chow hall. Most of the crew is still seasick and can't eat anything. But I don't miss a chow. It has cleared up this afternoon and the sea is getting calm. We are now making a pretty good speed.

November 9, 1944

It is very nice out this morning and the sea is very calm. It shouldn't take us so long to reach the states if the weather permits us to. Everyone is feeling fine this morning. Except I have another cold coming on me. This afternoon a Captain's Mast was held and there were about twenty fellows up before the captain including Dyson [William W. Dyson], De Cuir and myself. Mr. Davis rejoiced in seeing us there. But to his surprise the Captain dismissed our case. I am trying my best to keep from hitting Davis. But as soon as he gets smart with me, I am going to let him have it.

> [The captain's masts were courts at which the captain made decisions and meted out penalties for infractions of military law and rules. Dunn recalls that the captain often ended his masts by saying "Whatever you did, don't do it anymore. . . . Everything is dismissed." The captain maintained discipline, Dunn thinks, more by leadership than by masts.

James Graham (right) and Linden H. Kieffer (left)
take a break, sitting on the *Mason*'s smoke genera-
tors. Courtesy of James Graham.

Other crew members later made similar observations about how disci-
pline was maintained. Speaking to the sixth national convention of the
Destroyer-Escort Sailors Association held in Buffalo, New York, August 5–9, 1981, George D. Polk, who had been a radarman on board
the *Mason*, made the following comments:

"Lt. Cmdr. William M. Blackford, USNR, was the first skipper of
the USS *Mason*. {Blackford commanded the ship on all of its wartime
patrols. In mid-1945, he was promoted to other naval duties, and another officer took command of the *Mason*.} From time to time he was
subjected to sarcastic remarks from the other ship captains relative to
the fact that his crew was for the most part *black*. The following is
a true excerpt from one of such conversations as recorded by a war
correspondent:

' . . . Blackford, you must have somewhat of a problem with all of those niggers on your ship, and so few white men.'

Almost angrily, Captain Blackford responded, ' . . . Contrary to what you want to believe, I have *less* of a problem than you. We get along fine and do our jobs with no trouble of any sort. I regard my ship to be just like any of the hundreds of DEs on the high seas, *not as a problem child nor as an experiment. I am not a crusader, I am not trying to solve the race problem.* I am simply trying to run a good, Navy fighting ship. Actually, my men get into less trouble than those of other ships *because they know how to behave.'*

At this point, I would like to say for 'Big Bill,' as we among ourselves affectionately called him, and I wish he were present to hear me say this, as a crew, to a man, we would have probably followed him to HELL and back" {copy of talk in the editor's possession; see also *Buffalo News,* August 9, 1981}.]

November 10, 1944

It looks just like a July morning outside and all of us air our bedding. Things are just about the same except most of the boys dislike the way the ship is being run. Our friend Davis is the cause of a lot of it. I think the boys are going to take care of him when we hit port. There are submarines in our area but they haven't come close enough for us to attack any of them. We are trying to make it home before Thanksgiving and are making a good job so far. Someone took one of my small table lamps and I can't locate it at all. It is too late to make another. We should make it home in about eight more days.

November 11, 1944

This is another fine day and it is very warm. We are not doing much of anything but taking it easy. I am just about under the weather again. I'll be OK in a day or two. This afternoon we fired our large guns just to keep in practice. All you can see floating around the ship are books of nude women the boys picked up in England. You can imagine what they are saying. Even my good friend Denson is reading one of the books.

November 12, 1944

We are now passing the Azores and that means that it won't be long before reaching the states. I am feeling a little better today. The boys are either sleeping or playing cards and talking about each other. Just any little thing to occupy their minds. We had a very nice Bible discussion today. It was very interesting.

November 13, 1944

We were heading into a storm but it passed around us. Although it was a little rough. While standing watch on the bridge this morning a large swell came up over the bridge and just about washed me over the side. I was wet all over. And that didn't do my cold any good. This afternoon we are fifty miles behind the convoy because two of the tugs broke down. But we should catch them before reaching the states. Tubby, another signalman and myself were called to fire a 20 mm. gun in a contest in which a few of the officers participated. After summing up all of the scores Tubby and I won by three points. The Captain acted as judge.

November 14, 1944

The two tugs have finally got going again and we are only forty-one miles from the convoy. It is just like a summer day out, everyone is in their shirtsleeves. Another destroyer escort came back to relieve us today and we are now on our way to rejoin the convoy. We should pull into Norfolk Monday morning. There isn't anything of importance going on today. Our division doesn't have anything to do when not on watch. It's really too warm to sleep. Of

61

course Webb [probably Amos Webster] is working and also my good friend De Cuir. We are just off the coast of Bermuda, the land of sunshine.

November 15, 1944

We are steadily pushing toward home and should arrive next Wednesday or Thursday in New York. Our ship pulled up beside the oiler today and took on more fuel in about 25 minutes. They might not know it, but this crew is paving the way for other fellows to come. The Commodore of our task group is going to send a letter into Washington for citation on our good work that was done in the English Channel. I think that we are still going to make that movie. A fellow by the name of Stewart who works for Walt Disney was aboard and trying to plan for the picture.

> [Throughout his diary, Dunn showed a sense of the pathbreaking work of the *Mason's* men. He remarked at various points about how fast, how able, how good the crew was at accomplishing its tasks; and he compared his shipmates to white crews on other ships.
>
> The movie Dunn mentioned would be made. Titled *The Negro Sailor*, it was used by Mary Pat Kelly in her documentary video *Proudly We Served*.]

November 16, 1944

Since we are nearing the states, all of the boys' spirits are very high. Everyone is making plans and preparations for leave if we get any. My cold is much better and I am beginning to feel like myself once again. This is really a swell bunch of fellows to know aboard ship. Of course, you will always find some rotten ones in the group. But the boys usually get along fine. But I am afraid if they don't get Davis off of here something is going to happen to him.

November 17, 1944

This is a very dreary looking day and we are steadily pushing on. All of us are below deck doing the usual thing. There is a storm coming our way and we were told to prepare for a rough sea. It began to rain late this evening and the sea is getting rough. So I am hitting my sack for the night.

November 18, 1944

I went on watch at four o'clock in the morning and we are in a terrific storm. The ship is really tossing and the wind is blowing about sixty miles an hour. Around about five thirty day began to break and you could see swells coming up on all sides. They were forty five feet high. I was thrown against the bulkhead but it only shook me up a little and I cut my hand. All of the leave papers are being made out. Davis is still trying to make trouble for most of the boys aboard ship. I am going to whip him and go to the brig if he tries anything with me.

November 19, 1944

Well, the storm is letting up a little and we should be picking up speed. All of us have our papers waiting to be signed. A [leave] list was posted and my name wasn't on it. So I went to see my division officer and he told me that I couldn't have leave because of being A.W.O.L. in New York and England. I had a Captain's Mast once, but both charges were dismissed. They were not to be put in my records. Davis sneaks and puts them in anyway. I found out about it and asked to see my record and he tore something out of it which shouldn't have been in there. I am investigating it and if he did try to keep me from getting my leave, we are going to have [at] it. The convoy has split up and we have three ships which we are delivering to Norfolk and then we proceed to New York. If I don't get leave I am going anyway.

November 20, 1944

Today we ran into a hurricane and the wind is blowing sixty five miles an hour. We are constantly kept busy on the signal bridge. Everyone has to be careful when going topside. I am quite sure that we will be late getting in. My division officer found out that they had accused me wrong, so he told me everything was forgiven. So Mr. Davis lost again.

November 21, 1944

The storm is getting worse and we are losing speed. The three ships with us are having an awful time. We are just about lost ourselves, because we can't get our position from the sun and stars. About eleven o'clock tonight we found out where we were. We are just off the coast of Norfolk.

November 22, 1944

We delivered the three ships this morning at three and are now on our way to New York and it is still very rough. We arrived in N.Y. at 10:00 P.M. tonight and so ends another journey.

5

To Oran, Africa, and Back

December 18, 1944–February 11, 1945

In late December 1944 the Mason's convoy route changed. The ship had been escorting convoys between the United States and the United Kingdom in support of the Allied landings in northern France. As these landings succeeded—the last major German offensive in the West, the Battle of the Bulge, failed in December 1944—the Allies converged on Germany from all sides. For some time Allied forces had been fighting northward through Italy. Consequently, the Mason and other warships were needed to escort convoys to North Africa, a jumping-off place for supplies for the Allies in Italy and later in southern France. From December 1944 until the end of the war in Europe in May 1945, the Mason's job was to escort convoys from American ports to Oran, Algeria, a North African port just inside the Straits of Gibraltar. The ship set out from New York City on the first such convoy in mid-December 1944.

December 18, 1944

Today we are taking on ammunition and stores and everyone is very busy. This evening at five twenty we are pulling out from the pier and anchored outside of the channel.

[In a long letter to his parents written on December 18, Lt. Comdr. Blackford described his expectations for this trip. "We are preparing to take off again on a new adventure to a place I have never been, and one which should prove interesting in more ways than one. We are working for a good outfit now and I am looking forward to the job. . . . Have just completed a series of conferences with the Bureau of Personnel who are giving us every possible assistance with our problems. . . . Morale has been on the upswing for several months now, and I understand we have an excellent reputation for operations. The job is becoming increasingly more pleasurable. . . . The eventual policy for negro personnel has been finally decided upon, but I could not discuss it here. In any case we can expect to get more cooperation than in the past, which is good. . . . This is really a good job in all respects." It is unclear from this letter and navy records what "problems" the captain was referring to.

In his letter the captain mentioned leaving for a new adventure to a place he had not been before. In the interests of security, the crew members on the *Mason* and on other navy ships never knew beforehand where they were going. Only after the ship was at sea did the captain announce their destination.]

December 19, 1944

We lifted anchor at 4:30 this morning and are getting underway with another convoy whose destination is North Africa. We met the other division of the convoy from New York and now we have 70 some Liberty ships with supplies to deliver to N. Africa.

[Liberty ships were mass-produced freighters designed to carry goods to Allied armies.]

December 22, 1944

This is our fourth day out and we are making good speed. It's the same old thing so I won't bother to write it down. We received a message last night saying that one destroyer and one destroyer escort had been hit near the Azores at 10:00 A.M. So we are headed that way and have to be very careful. We are supposed to hit Morocco, Algiers, Oran, Naples, Bizzentia, Casablanca, Gibraltar and Cairo.

[It is unclear from navy records whether either a destroyer or destroyer escort was in fact hit.]

December 24, 1944

This a beautiful Sunday, the sun is shining and it is just like a summer day. Today is Xmas Eve and we are having a party. All of the boys are on the stern of the ship with our small tree and it is decorated very pretty. We have a band called the Sea Jam Five and a vocalist. They are really good. Everyone enjoyed the party very much. We had plenty of nuts, candy and some of us had egg nog. We have fifty cases of beer aboard and are going to have another party ashore when we reach Africa. The moon is really pretty at night and it is too warm for jackets.

[Dunn remembers that the band included a pianist, a saxophone player, a trumpet player, and several singers. "We were having a good time."]

December 25, 1944

Well, De Cuir and Bootsie [James N. Shores] greeted me early this morning before the others had gotten up. But I happened to be awake when they came. Today is just like yesterday only it is warmer. DuFau and I sent out Xmas greetings to the other ships this morning by light and also received quite a few of them. We had our Xmas dinner at 1:00 P.M. today and it was a very nice one with turkey, dressing, sweet potatoes, lettuce, olives, cigars, cigarettes, cake, pie and ice cream. The only thing lacking was ham and Jane. The boys are all standing around trying to see what I am writing. But I got them covered.

December 31, 1944

Everything is going along fine aboard ship. It has been a beautiful day and tonight the moon is very bright. We are waiting for the New Year. At midnight all of us joined in singing Auld Lang Syne. Later some of us got together and went into the kitchen. We stole some alcohol and mixed it together with eggs and other things and had plenty of egg nog. That was one way of celebrating the New Year.

January 4, 1945

The German subs are really on the loose. Another ship was sunk last night up ahead of us. And tonight we received an urgent message saying that five ships had been sunk outside of the Straits of Gibraltar. We finally got thru without any trouble and now we are passing the rock of Gibraltar and it is really a large one and well fortified.

January 5, 1945

We are now entering Oran, North Africa and it is very cold. Our ship pulled up to the dock and we saw Arabs and Frenchmen. They wore those turbans on their heads. The Germans had this city at one time. The boys and I went on liberty and the Arabs don't have much clothing and you can sell anything to wear. One fellow wanted to buy my coat. Everything is very high. We drank some cognac and it made some of the boys just about crazy. All of the boys did not get liberty. Some got souvenirs and some didn't.

January 6, 1945

We pulled out of port Saturday night and dropped anchor for the night. This morning we are waiting for a convoy to form. Its destination is New York. There are 25 ships in the convoy and we will probably arrive in New York on the 26 of Jan. So we have seen North Africa, and I am wondering where our next convoy will go after leaving the states again. The subs will probably be waiting for us to come out of Gibraltar but we are prepared to deal with them.

January 12, 1945

Well, it is nice outside today and we really had a scare last night. Around about 12:30 last night we picked up a contact on our sound gear and thought it to be a sub. The captain gave orders to stand by to drop depth charges. But we passed over it first and then circled it. Then we decided to ram it. Everyone was on needles and pins. All of a sudden we hit it and dropped depth charges at once. You could hear the Capt. say "Fire one, fire two and so on." After attacking we came back to see what was floating in the water. We thought we had survivors but found out that it was a barge. We crippled our ship and had to leave the convoy. We are on our way to Bermuda. Some of the boys really prayed that night. But had it been a sub we would have blown it to bits. These boys are really on the ball. The Capt. congratulated them on their alertness. Now they are listening to all the fine [phonograph] records. If you used your imagination, you would think that you were in New York at a bar. That's how the music makes you feel.

[Many of the men on ship later speculated that the *Mason* may have hit one of the barges abandoned from Convoy N.Y. 119 the previous fall. Ocean currents could have carried the barge this far south. The *Mason's* War Diary for February 11 recorded the event as follows: "At 0015 made radar contact bearing 140 degrees distance 1500 yards. Sound contact was made on the same bearing at 1200 yards. This 'pip' bore such remarkable resemblance to periscopes seen during training exercises that the decision was made to attack. . . . All hands manned battle stations, full speed was rung up, and depth charges were set on 50 feet. . . . A heavy shock was felt forward, speed was not materially reduced and charges were dropped. . . . Lookouts reported wreckage floating down both sides of the ship. . . . Illumination by searchlight revealed plainly that the target was a wooden derelict, probably a barge about 100 feet by 50 feet."

This incident points out the imprecision of antisubmarine warfare in World War II. It was not always possible for sonar operators to distinguish submarines from whales, barges, and other objects, which resulted in many false attacks.]

January 14, 1945

Everyone is just about back to normal again after such a scare last week. All of us are going to celebrate our Xmas and New Year as soon as we reach the states if possible. We are just hobbling along now since our ship has been damaged. Some good news came in today. We received orders to proceed to New York instead of Bermuda and we really rejoiced at that. I would have been second class [signalman's rating] if I had not been late in New York last time. But I would do it again to be with Jane.

January 20, 1945

Steaming as before with #1 and #2 engines going full speed ahead. Our [compass] course 288 [degrees], with #3 and #4 engines out, our port shaft is also out. Destination New York. We pulled into Bermuda Thursday night. Friday morning a diver went down to look at our shafts and rudders which were in bad shape. The captain and other officers went ashore and came back drunk. But the crew had to remain aboard. A couple of the chiefs got drunk and had a fight last night. The crew were also pretty high but the captain can't understand where the whiskey came from. De Cuir and myself just finished a bottle of V.O. They should know that they can't outsmart the crew. And now he can't understand why half the crew was drunk last night. They are trying to find some whiskey aboard but it's all gone now. We should arrive in N.Y. at 8:00 A.M. Monday morning.

Laying a depth charge from the *Mason*. Courtesy of James Graham.

January 22, 1945

We arrived in New York this morning and docked at Earl, N.J. to unload all of our ammunition. We finished unloading about 1:00 P.M. and then came into the Brooklyn Navy yard. And so ends another successful trip over and back again.

February 2, 1945

On this day we left New York for Earl, N.J. to pick up ammunition. The harbor was filled with ice and we had difficulty in reaching Earl, N.J. but finally arrived there OK. We began to load ammunition at eleven o'clock and finished at eight tonight. We are now getting underway for Block Island just outside of Newport, N.J. We were very disappointed because we were under the impression that we would go back to New York. But it just goes to show that you can never plan on anything in the Navy. I know that we are headed for another long trip in the South Atlantic. And we probably end up in Africa once more. Jimmy fell thru a hatch and is lying in bed with an injured leg. Of course he can jive the man now [that is, get off work]. Everything worked out fine for me last nite.

February 3, 1945

It is very cold this morning and I went on watch at four o'clock. The wind is howling all around me and the sea is raging. The decks are slippery and one had to be very careful that he doesn't slip over the side, because you would freeze to death. There is ice all over the ship and it is something like you see in the movies and read about. We are practicing with an American sub and will not get any liberty in New London, Conn. The crew is pretty tired after working hard yesterday but they will be back to normal in a few days. We arrived off of Block island at nine o'clock and the sub was waiting for us. It's a great life if you don't weaken. After staying out all day with the sub we finally dropped anchor in Block island sound for the night. And so ends our first day of maneuvers.

February 4, 1945

This morning at seven thirty we got underway to meet the sub for more practice. The weather was a little nippy but we had to go anyway. The sun with her extravagant rays shining down on us, we proceeded with our maneuvers. With the beautiful surroundings of Mother Nature all around us we didn't mind it so much. The sub submerged and we contacted it by code. The boys in that department can't read it so well by ear and they called for a signalman and a radio man which was myself and Peters [Merwin Peters]. I had read most of it when he arrived. After completing our exercises we went into Long Island Sound and it was covered with ice. Our Capt. tried to take it in but the ship just slid and now we are returning to Block island where we will anchor for tonight.

Good evening friends.

February 5, 1945

Another day has dawned and we are getting underway for more exercises with the sub. Four more ships in the division joined our exercises this morning. The beach was covered with snow this morning although it is not as cold as usual. We had a little party last night eating canned pears, pineapples, salad dressing, potted meat and crackers. We stayed out until three thirty this evening and then returned to our usual anchorage. De Cuir and I are sitting here talking of different things. The boys are buying many cartons of cigarettes to bring back home. I think we will leave for Oran, Algeria in Africa some time soon but you know that we are due back in April. Well, I guess that I will attend the movie tonight and then turn in. Good night.

February 6, 1945

We got underway as usual this morning and the temperature is just about the same although some ice is still along the coast line. There are about seven ships in our company and two submarines. None of the ships have granted liberty to any of the boys as yet and probably won't. Jones, DuFau, Buck and myself were very busy on the signal bridge this morning. We had quite a few flag signals and it was all we could do was to take care of all the traffic including the light. Several planes came over also and we operated with them for awhile. Yeoman Grant is going back to New York to the hospital and he will probably miss this trip. We finally finished our exercise and are now returning to our anchorage for the night.

February 7, 1945

As usual we are getting underway at seven thirty this morning for our usual exercise with submarines and planes. The sub went under and we began to make runs on it just as we would in battle. We made several direct hits. It wasn't so bad out today because the weather has opened up a little since yesterday. We finished our exercises about three o'clock this afternoon and the sub came up and headed for its berth. We came back to the usual place and dropped anchor. Grant left on one of the other ships for New York. We will leave for Norfolk tomorrow. The boys are shooting craps in the shower and I am trying to write. The lights are out. So this ends another day.

February 8, 1945

It has begun to snow this morning at seven thirty and we are getting underway. They have canceled our exercises with the submarines due to bad weather. We are waiting around to see how the weather is going to turn out. All of us want to go to New York but we know what the story is at present. Most of us are below talking about different things. Finally we are on our way to Norfolk, Va. and should arrive at noon tomorrow. The weather is letting up now and it looks fairly good outside. We are steadily forging ahead toward Norfolk and you should see the boys shining their shoes and getting their uniforms pressed. Well, this just about covers everything for the day and I am now turning in for the night.

February 9, 1945

We arrived in Norfolk about twelve o'clock today and the weather was just like a spring day. Our section had liberty and De Cuir and I went out and had a few drinks together. Later I called my mother and it was good to know that she was getting along fine. There isn't anything to do in Norfolk and the whiskey is six and seven dollars a pint. We only stayed out a few hours and then returned to the ship. The boys never like to go on liberty here because someone might say something to them about sitting up front on a street car and then it would be a fight. We never stay over two or three days at the most.

To Oran, Africa, and Back

February 10, 1945

Today is very nice and warm. Most of the boys have little odd jobs
to do aboard ship. Our basketball team has a game with Hampton
Institute [an African American college in Virginia modeled on the
Tuskegee Institute] this afternoon and a dance afterwards. I have
the duty today but my division officer let me go play with the team.
Around about two o'clock we left the ship and arrived at Hampton
about three thirty. The game started immediately. We put out a
nice exhibition after being off of the court for such a long time. The
game ended in a tie so they didn't play it off and the score remained
in a deadlock. Some of the boys stayed for the dance, but De Cuir
and myself left since there were mostly kids on the campus. We had
a few drinks and returned to the ship.

February 11, 1945

When I awakened this morning my muscles felt as though they had
been through a grinding machine. I am sore all over. This is another beautiful day and everyone is walking around in their shirt
sleeves. There is no liberty today because we are supposed to leave.
Several shipmates and myself went out on the base to the canteen
and had a beer and then played several games of pool. We returned
to the ship about three o'clock. At four we pulled out of Norfolk
and anchored. We saw a fairly good movie and then retired for the
night.

6

To Oran Again

February 12–March 7, 1945

Escorting convoys to Oran became almost a shuttle run for the Mason's *crew. On their seventh crossing of the Atlantic they left Norfolk headed again for Oran. Once there, they enjoyed an extensive shore leave.*

February 12, 1945

At four fifteen this morning they sounded reveille and we had to rise. Our chow was served at five and we got under way at five thirty. We are to meet the convoy that we are taking to Africa. I have been on watch all morning and the convoy hasn't come out yet. I have just awakened from a nice nap and it is time for evening chow. The convoy has formed and we are on our way with about thirty-five ships and one destroyer, three destroyer escorts and one frigate headed for an unknown destination as far as we know. All of the boys seem to be satisfied because they and myself feel that we will return to the states soon to see our loved ones once again. Well, I am going on watch for four hours and then retire to my sack until morning.

February 13, 1945

It is a bad morning out. It is raining pretty hard and the wind is strong. We have been expecting this for a couple of days. Buck and

I are on the signal bridge together. We finally go inside for awhile and all of a sudden we see a flashing light. It is one of the ships calling us. It is pouring down rain outside. I received the message and Buck wrote it down. Of all times to get a long message was then. It had sixty-five words. By the time we finished the two of us were drenched. I finished my noon chow and read "True Confession" magazine all afternoon. We look on the map and found out that we were going to France. It should be a long and tough trip for us.

February 14, 1945

Well here we are about one thousand miles from the states for Valentine's day and here is a valentine that I composed for Jane. It is not much but she will know I haven't forgotten.

Of all the gals that I ever knew,
I was right when I married you,
And I have sailed the ocean far and wide,
But have found nothing on the other side.
Now believe me my dear this is not just a line,
You're my everlasting valentine.

We are proceeding on to our destination. The weather is beginning to break and is getting much warmer. We will case Bermuda tomorrow. Nothing of importance has happened as yet. And now I shall finish my reading and sleeping. So good night, my sweet, and say a little prayer for all of us.

February 15, 1945

The sea is still rough and we are trying our best to go around this storm. But we keep running into another one. We can't sleep very well at night because when the ship rolls we have to hold on to keep from falling out of our sacks. We have been in rough weather ever since we left Norfolk last Monday. We have been taking it sort of easy on this trip. That's why I read quite a bit to keep my mind occupied. Our chows are a lot better on this trip because the officers sample it before we eat it. We haven't run into anything as yet. An empty raft was seen floating by today and we decided to use it for target practice. We fired several shots at it to no avail. So now I must get back to my reading. Good night.

February 16, 1945

Well the sea hasn't let up very much because it was just like the night before. I awakened this morning and took a nice hot and cold shower and it made me feel real good. Of course Bootsie and I have had our usual friendly argument. His sack is next to mine and we get in each other's way while dressing. And Jimmy [James Thomas] never sleeps in his sack. We have to argue with him about our sacks. He says Bootsie and I are like two old women powdering up and using cosmetics. But we have to keep our schoolboy complexions and physique. We had a letter from St. James and he is doing OK and should be out very soon. Webb is playing pinochle and he is raising hell. De Cuir is sleeping as usual and if some one doesn't wake him for chow he will have a fit. He is a spoiled boy. Well that is all for today. Will be back in a dash with a flash.

Dear Jane,

I can write this without any doubts in my mind at all. I love you very much and always have, but I guess I never acted much like it at times. I don't have but two things in this world to live for and that's you and mother. And, I will love you until I die. Darling, I miss you very much but I know there will come a day when we can settle down once more. Our life was just like a story that I just finished, but I am glad that I got a hold of myself before it was too late. Love you, my darling, with all my heart. Yours Always, your devoted hubby Jimmy.

Transferring mail to the *Mason*. Courtesy of James Graham.

I was just reading some of your old letters and the admiral really acted up. You know he is very sensitive (smiles).

I am trying to get transferred off this even though I would miss my friends. But it's to no advantage that I stay on here any longer. The other signalman Buck and myself can't advance at all because second class is closed. Our officer lied to us.

Darling, I can picture our little home with all of the conveniences in it for us. I don't exactly know where it will be but in some nice city. I miss you more and more as the days go by and love you the same way. If you only knew just how heavy my heart is at this very moment. But I can take it. Because I have you to look forward to seeing and also mother. I would go thru hell to reach you two. If a corset cover covers a corset, what does the corset cover? Give up! A milk dairy, naval station, pleasure resort, and a crap source.

February 17, 1945

The old sea is still acting up and we haven't had a nice calm day as yet. But we are steadily pushing forward to our destination. Most of us are getting restless and want to get a transfer although we know that this is our best bet. We are all sitting around on my sack and others writing letters or reading. Just something to keep our minds occupied. I was just reading a letter from a shipmate of mine who was transferred last August. He is stationed now on one of the islands in the South Pacific and he said that we were lucky. He also told me that Price and Ed Masterson were with him. Two boys from home. Well, we are still holding on hoping that this war will soon come to an end.

February 18, 1945

Well, here we are again a few hundred miles nearer our destination and nothing has happened as yet. All of us seem to be in a good mood today although it is raining and the sea is still rough as ever. I have actually gotten more sleep on this trip than on any of the others. De Cuir, Jimmie, Bootsie and myself had our little chat about different things as usual today. At chow time all of the latest records were being played over the P.A. system and the boys began talking about the Mandalay Bar. Of course we thought of our wives and girl friends. That's something you do every day. It is thrilling at times convoying ships because we know that men and women and children are waiting on materials that we are bringing to them and the mail must get through at any cost.

February 19, 1945

Still steaming at fourteen knots screening the convoy as usual. Last night was a very beautiful one. It was the best one that we have had on this trip. Today is cloudy and the sea is still rough. We have been at sea one week today and it seems like a month. Of course the first week always seems like that. As usual I slept all morning and got up just in time for noon chow. I haven't seen De Cuir all day. He must sleep some place. The admiral tried to act up this morning but I finally got him quieted down after I went to sleep. We are planning on having a big softball game when we reach Africa with one of the other ships and you know that this is right up my alley.

February 20, 1945

Well, my sweet, today is your birthday and I am thousands of miles out at sea. Wish I could be with you to celebrate but I am thinking of you all the while. I hope you have a very happy birthday. Everything is just about the same aboard ship. We saw a movie yesterday afternoon and it was pretty good. Two boys started to fight in the chow hall but they were stopped. But one of the boys later took a wrench and knocked the other boy in the head and nothing has been done as yet. Two officers got into an argument today and one of them walked off from his duty. I don't know what will happen next. Webb and De Cuir beat me playing pinochle and they are really riding me good. But I will get them. This is a day of happenings. Happy birthday.

Darling,

I really miss you especially today because we could have had a lovely time just together. I love you so much that it's a damn shame and so does the admiral (smiles). But don't let your head get too big (smiles). I would love to give you a present today, but it will keep for you. A trip home would be a good one, plus the admiral and all of you wanted of him (smiles). I will stop that nonsense now because he is acting up a little. I will try to find you something nice in Africa or France. How do you like this? Our love is just like the birds, trees, and the weather. We were really meant for each other and finally drawn together. It wasn't because of me and not because of you. It was the Lord because he really knew, but as the

81

time lingers on and we are far apart, I still have you tucked away safely in my heart.

> So now you can clearly see,
> What you really mean to me,
> And now from the bottom of my heart,
> I really must say,
> I wish you very happy and pleasant birthday.
>   James Dunn.

February 21, 1945

For the first time on this trip today is turning out to be a lovely one and the sea has calmed down quite a bit. We were warned to be alert for subs at the entrance of Gibraltar. We are six days out of Algeria. I think we are going to France from there. So you know what I will be thinking. I caught Webb and De Cuir last night and wore them out playing pinochle and I really did ride them. We are following the usual routine aboard ship. The results of the argument between the [chief petty] officers yesterday was sort of bad because the Captain is having one of them transferred when we return to the states. So this is about all for today. Except we're seeing another movie, "Song to Remember."

February 22, 1945

On this birthday of one of our great statesmen and presidents of the U.S. [George Washington], we are trying to accomplish the same thing he was fighting for. We are steaming ahead at 13 knots on this beautiful day. Most of us worked this morning at odd jobs and didn't mind at all. I am trying to write and Bootsie keeps after me. I saw a lovely movie last night. "The Song to Remember." It was the story of Chopin during his early childhood and up through his manhood. He was Polish and a brilliant pianist who died young. Well, we are going to have a general quarters in a few minutes so I must be on my way.

February 23, 1945

This is another nice day and we are passing the Azores just off the coast of Portugal. Today all of us had to take our canvass off of bunks and wash them. We are getting prepared for an inspection by an admiral. Not our admiral (smiles). All of the boys seem to be going about their work today without any argument. Webb is having an awful time getting some of the boys to work in his division. I would hate to have you listen to him swear. Bootsie and I have finished and are lying in our sacks to get our rest before going on watch this evening. All of us are stocking up on cigarettes. My friend Fred [Denson] is worrying himself sick about his wife. I try to console him but I guess he is still childish. Well, I guess that we will reach our destination next week and nothing has happened yet.

February 24, 1945

Ah! What a lovely day to be at sea. You can see the sun coming up and setting on the horizon. It is really a beautiful sight to see. Everyone aboard ship seems to be very busy these days making preparations for our annual inspection. I think all of us will be painters when we get out of this Navy since we specialize in it aboard ship. Yesterday afternoon a merchant marine fell over the side of his ship and one of the fellows happened to see him in time. So one of the escorts went back to pick him up. Had it been at night he would never have been found. Webb is still raising hell with his boys. Bootsie is sleeping and De Cuir is dodging work as usual. And we all hope to be back in the states in time for the Easter parade.

Handling a shell for one of the 3″ guns. Courtesy of James Graham.

February 25, 1945

Our convoy is still all together this fine Sunday afternoon and the crews are all in good shape although a little excitement happened yesterday afternoon. One of the ships picked up a submarine near the convoy and before we knew anything we were dropping depth charges. After the attack we waited for something to appear on the surface of the water but nothing appeared. Evidently we hit him or it got away. We really need some excitement. The boys were at their battle stations in nothing flat. We are supposed to pick up a Captain in Gibraltar and take him to France but our orders change so quickly that we never know what's coming up next. De Cuir and Webb are worrying me about playing pinochle so I must stop and give them a few lessons.

To Oran Again

February 26, 1945

It is a beautiful morning but a little cool. All of our compartments are being painted by the crew. Our division is painting today but I am on watch this morning and the boys said that they knew I would have something else to do at the time. We are having a trial aboard ship and it is an interesting case. A watch was stolen and also some money. They don't know exactly who did it but they have a suspect. And now they have several boys mixed up in it. They are having regular investigations and questionings. The suspect has a lawyer. And we also have a prosecuting atty. and the Captain acting as the judge. It reminds you of a great robbery trying to be solved by Scotland Yard. Well, the boys finished painting this evening and the place looks pretty good.

February 27, 1945

This is a beautiful morning with the sun coming up over the horizon and the moon going down. We were up early this morning and on the alert for enemy submarines. They are very dangerous in these parts. We will be entering the Straits of Gibraltar at midnight and the subs usually hang right outside the straits for convoys. We received a distress signal from some ship near there and she was sinking but we were too far away to aid her. The skipper wants to get a sub very badly. We will also man our battle stations this evening before sunset. That's when they usually attack. But we will be waiting for them when they arrive and will entertain them for a while. Well, after such a strenuous day I will resume my sleeping.

February 28, 1945

Last night at twelve o'clock we entered the channel entrance to Gibraltar without encountering any enemy submarines although we had expected to see a few. The wind and sea began to act up as we were entering and submarines are no trouble at all in rough

85

weather. The Lord was taking care of us. But little did the officers think of this. I was on watch [unclear] as we passed the great rock of Gibraltar at five o'clock this morning. The moon was very bright and the skies were clear. I watched the sun come up and the moon go down and it was a beautiful sight. Today is very beautiful and we can see Spain and Africa. We didn't make our trip to France due to the lack of fuel. But we will arrive in Oran, Algeria, in the morning. This will end another successful trip.

March 1, 1945

Everything seems to be going fine today. We are in the Mediterranean Sea and it is very beautiful. Everyone is still busy getting ready for our inspection. We and two escorts are on our way to Oran, Algeria. We are in charge of them. Last night while on watch one of the lookouts on another ship reported a scream was heard in the water and we searched for about two hours without success. We arrived in Oran, Algeria, this morning and the weather is very nice. Our mail came through today and I didn't receive any mail from my wife. You know how I felt. But later I found out that all letters have to be sent by air mail in order for you to receive them at your next port. Well, it won't be long before I'll be back in the states. Just a matter of weeks.

March 2, 1945

It is much warmer out today and the sun is really burning down. I had to take some shots the other day and my arm is still sore. We get the shots yearly. Things seem to be very quiet around this place but you can see them moving big guns on up the line. Today I was designated as one of the S.P.s (Shore Patrols) and our officers gave us a Billy [club] and .45 automatic pistol. We went into the city and were stationed at our assigned posts. I was asked a million questions by Arabs, Jews, Africans, French and Spanish women, men, and children. They had never seen a Negro S.P. and they were very nice. They like the American Negro but not whites. This was a wonderful experience. We were finished at nine thirty tonight and returned to the ship without having any trouble.

[In recalling shore leave in Oran, Dunn says that "Oran was nice." The streets were off-limits, "but a lot of cats would find a way to go."]

March 3, 1945

This is a beautiful day and our ship is ready for inspection which will be held Monday morning. We will probably leave next Thursday and should arrive on the 28th of March just before Easter. Today I have liberty and am going to try to pick up a few souvenirs. Webb, Bootsie and a couple of other fellows went on liberty and didn't get out until seven o'clock. We had several drinks. Later we walked around and the kids worried us crazy to buy souvenirs and they want a fortune for them. Liberty is up at ten o'clock so we came on back to the ship. Denson was on S.P. duty tonight and he was just telling us about the way they worried him as they did me last night. And what surprised me, Denson took a drink of cognac.

March 4, 1945

Everyone was up bright and early on this lovely Sunday morning although it is cooler than usual. The Captain inspected our ship this morning and it seems to be in good shape. There isn't any liberty at all today because of inspection tomorrow. The lights are supposed to go out at eight o'clock tonight. Our chow today was delicious. We had chicken, cream peas, sweet potatoes, soup, and cherry ice cream. One of my boy friends by the name of Jimmy Thomas is sick and had to stay over here in the hospital for a while. All of us hate to leave him because he is a swell guy. We played a little football and softball after chow and then retired for the afternoon.

CHAPTER 6

March 5, 1945

Well, we are getting up at four o'clock this morning. Inspection started at eight thirty. The ship looks like new again. The Commodore looked over the ship and said it was the best ship of our group. The inspection was over at eleven thirty this morning and our Capt. granted liberty at one o'clock. De Cuir and I went out and shopped. When we were finished we bought a bottle of cognac and we went to a movie to drink it. I saw "This Is the Army, Mr. Jones." Afterwards we hired a buggy and took a ride in the country with two bottles. After about two hours we came back to the city and came back to the ship. Every street in Oran is off limits for service men. And the S.P.s are there to see that you don't get off limits.

March 6, 1945

We got underway at seven forty five this morning and I slept until noon. After chow I went on watch. At two thirty we fired all of our guns at a sleeve [a target] that was being towed by an airplane. We shot two of them down. We came in about five o'clock and the Capt. declared liberty. This is the last liberty because we are leaving for the states Thursday morning. Webb, Dyson, De Cuir and myself went on liberty together. We didn't get in town until eight o'clock and had a few drinks and had to start back at nine o'clock. When we arrived back to the ship everyone aboard was just about drunk and they had plenty of cognac and wine. It is eleven thirty and they are still raising hell. One of the white boys off of the ship next to us knocked an officer in the head with a brick and he was very drunk. They are quieting down a little now.

March 7, 1945

This is just like a July day in the states. It is very warm, in fact it is hot. Most of the fellows got up this morning with hangovers. But there isn't much work to be done. We swept our compartment and slept until chow. Webb has gone to town with 2,000 francs, which is forty dollars in American money. Most of us went on a beer party and the boys stopped on the way back and bought some cherry brandy, and I know there will be another drinking party aboard tonight. Webb came back loaded with souvenirs and almost drunk. He had just about everything imaginable. And he is selling it just like a black jew. We are leaving in the morning and all of us are very happy. Jimmy is in the hospital and De Cuir is walking the ship right now with a bottle of cherry brandy.

[The men were able to get good exchange rates, Dunn recalls, when changing francs for dollars. They were eager to do so and then send the dollars home to America. By "black jew," Dunn explains that he meant "a wheeler-dealer," a person who would "bargain."]

7

Returning to New York City

March 8–26, 1945

With the men cooped up on their small destroyer escort, tensions mounted on the return to the United States. As was typical of most ships' crews in the navy, conflicts developed on the Mason *the longer she was at sea. On this convoy, splits became pronounced, since a Jewish officer sympathized with some of the enlisted men who thought they were not being treated properly.*

March 8, 1945

We lifted anchor this morning and got underway with our convoy, which consisted of thirty ships, and we are headed for the United States. Of course I slept all morning until chow. Later I played a little tonk [a card game] for a dollar with several of the boys. I went on watch at four o'clock and found out that one of the boys had fallen into a gasoline tank aboard one of the merchant ships. About six thirty he died from suffocation. Tomorrow all ships will halfmast their colors for three hours and he will be buried at sea. All of the fellows seem to be in a good mood because they know that they are going home. And most of us will get a leave. We are still in the Mediterranean Sea with a tropical moon and the fragrance of jungle flowers while the couples in Oran slip away from the crowds to make love under her extravagant beam. What a life.

90

Darling Jane,

You don't know how I have longed for you, want to hold you close to me, and feel the warmth of your breath upon my face. How I wish you could have been with me under this magnificent moon. You were with me honey, but if you had only been there in flesh this would have been my paradise. But I know that it won't be long before I see you. And I pray that the Lord will keep you and my mother safe for me always. Darling, I love you more than words can express it and shall always love you. And by the way the admiral says the same things go for him and he is standing up just like a soldier. He says that's all he lives for, just to satisfy you. I am on my way.

March 9, 1945

Steaming as before on this lovely morning. Everyone was up at six thirty and quite a few of us took hot and cold showers. I felt like a boy of seventeen this morning. All of the ships halfmasted their colors at nine o'clock. I was on watch and I attended to ours. They buried him about ten and proceeded onward. We passed the rock of Gibraltar and Spanish Morocco and this is a very little city. It reminds you of the small cities you read about in mythology while in high school. We have a dog aboard for our mascot. He is a little black Scottish terrier and we call him Blackie. He is standing on the opposite bunk watching me write. The radio is playing and the music is soft and caressing. We can hardly wait to get home. We have entered the mad Atlantic and it is still rough.

[Not everyone liked the dog, for crew members had to clean up after him. At one point the dog either fell or was thrown overboard. Learning of this, the captain reversed course and picked up the dog, who was swimming toward New York City.

Submarines remained a problem in the Straits of Gibraltar. The *Mason*'s War Diary for March 9 records a typical encounter. "At 1700 GULFPORT reported sonar contact. MASON and GULFPORT both made embarrassing attacks and made a retiring search for two

91

hours without further contact." "Embarrassing" here means that the attacks embarrassed the submarines and scared them away from the convoy.]

March 10, 1945

The convoy is doing a good speed on this beautiful day and if the weather continues to stay like this we will be pulling into the states in about fifteen days. All of us are riding De Cuir about not going home on his leave. He says that he is not going to stop by and see his girl friend Lilla in New York. He is really weak for her but doesn't want us to know it. The Captain had an inspection yesterday and found things in very good shape in our compartment. We are supposed to be the brain and the pride of the ship (C-Division). We are passing the danger area but hasn't anything happened as yet. All of us are constantly on the lookout for submarines. U.S. planes are also covering the convoy. They just contacted two subs but lost them. I am not worried about my income taxes.

March 11, 1945

Well, there isn't very much to talk about because everything remains just about the same. We go through our regular routine daily. Today is a little cloudy and looks like rain but none has fallen as yet. All of us are just taking things easy and wishing that we were home. Upon our arrival we are going to try to get De Cuir and his girl friend Lilla married. He wants to get married but he just hates to give in. Last night we saw a movie entitled "The Adventures of Mark Twain," and I really enjoyed it very much. Today we saw "The Song of Bernadette" and it was an ideal Sunday movie. The general alarm just sounded and I jumped out of my sack and was the first on the signal bridge. Another destroyer escort dropped depth charges and we followed in behind them and did likewise. But, we didn't see anything. We searched for two hours.

March 12, 1945

All are well and we are still afloat. We have just about covered one thousand miles today and should be passing the Azores tomorrow. This morning I took another hot and cold shower. Of course the fresh water is on twice a day and I take a shower every other day. I was relaxing when all of a sudden one of my shipmates by the name of Townsend came up to my sack and asked for a drink of cognac which he knew was in my locker. I tried to stall him off because I wanted to take it home. But I finally weakened and gave him a small drink. And then up pops Bootsie. Well, you know the results. The day went by very fast and nothing has happened of any importance. I was on watch all afternoon and slept in the sun most of the time.

March 13, 1945

It is around six thirty and I have been on watch since four o'clock. The sun is very pretty rising on the horizon. It looks like a large Florida orange. I had my chow at seven forty five and retired for a while. The weather is warm and the water is sky blue. And it makes your heart yearn for the one you love. That's if you're a dreamer or sentimental. We received a message from New York stating that we would have an inspection upon arrival. But I hope it doesn't interfere with our leave. We are still playing pinochle quite a bit just to pass the time. This is just about all for today so I will go to the movie to see "The Fleet is In." Good night.

March 14, 1945

Steaming as before with number one and three engines on the line, speed 15 knots. This is another beautiful day and it is very warm. An American oiler came out from the Azores and we refueled at sea. It took about thirty minutes to fill our tanks. The usual thing is happening. Most of us are playing cards or sleeping. I had to stop writing for awhile because the boys were having an argument. It all started over some movies. The crew was supposed to see a movie tonight and the first class petty officers had it shown in their quarters and wouldn't let anyone else in. At the time De Cuir was asleep and Bootsie and I were playing pinochle. We finished our game and began to argue for the behalf of the crew. Of course, the first class petty officers didn't like it but we showed them two fine points and they couldn't deny it.

March 15, 1945

Today we resumed our little argument. We try to show them that we were being segregated enough at present by the white man. And they should be trying to better conditions for everybody instead of doing exactly what the white man wants to do. We have an officer aboard who is Jewish and the other officers don't like him. Of course, he tries to look out for the boys aboard ship. They have got his papers all made out for a transfer. I think he is writing a letter to Washington to expose the whole outfit. Things are not what people think they are aboard ship. They give authority to some of the fellows who have never had an opportunity nor a good education. And this fellow will run to the man [the Captain] with everything he hears. It is really pathetic. But things will change sooner or later.

> [Dunn describes the Jewish officer as "a nice fellow" who was "jolly" and who "loved sports." He would "mingle with the fellows and keep us up on everything. . . . He talked the same way the crew would talk." Some of the other officers did not like him "because he was too close to the crew."]

March 16, 1945

We are just about seven days out of New York this morning and the convoy is still going strong although one ship had to take another route because it couldn't keep up with the rest. It is much better aboard ship as far as water is concerned. It is left on at all times for

Roosevelt Luster and Leroy Booker, two crew members, relax between watches. Courtesy of James Graham.

the use of the crew. All of us put ourselves in the laundry today to be cleaned and pressed because we should get in New York next Friday. Last night the Commodore had all the ships go to general quarters for a drill. He wanted to test the speed of each ship. We were ready in 42 seconds which was 8 seconds faster than the Navy requires and 2 min. faster than any other ship. The Commodore sent a message saying that all ships were too slow. I took the message to the Captain and he was mad enough to fight. And he sent a message back to the Commodore.

March 17, 1945

It's eleven o'clock this morning and I just got up. It is a beautiful day out and the water is like a large flow of blue ink. I stand two watches during 24 hours and the rest of the time I just lounge about someplace. Bootsie just came in and he is after me again. De Cuir is laid up in his sack resting. He told the man that he was ill and they put him to bed. He says that he is living the life of a king. It is time for chow so excuse me a moment. I ate my noon chow and had to go upon the signal bridge to paint some letters in our flag bag. I got back about eight o'clock and started to play pinochle. The lights went out at nine. I washed my face, put cream on and then took a small shot of cognac. And now I have a flashlight on to finish my writing. So now I guess I'll call it a day.

March 18, 1945

Not only is today Passion Sunday, but every day when I'm thinking of you darling. It is very pretty out today and we are only five days out of New York. I imagine that it is nice in the states today. Everything is quiet aboard ship today. Most of us are sleeping or writing. We had a very lovely dinner today, fried chicken, noodles, asparagus tips, soup and cake for dessert. The officer I mentioned a few pages back is really going to expose the officers aboard ship. It might not do any good, but it will give Washington something to think about. All of the officers are worried about the matter. Because all of them were drunk in Bermuda on our last trip back to the states. If we had been attacked by submarines, they would not have been any use to us at all. So we will wait and see what the outcome is going to be.

March 19, 1945

It is a bright beautiful morning with the sun coming up on the horizon in back of us. We are getting closer to home each day and we are four days out of New York. My name was on the leave list today and our leave will start upon arrival in the states. Webster is going home with me. Today was pay day aboard ship and the boys are indulging a little. Although I was in a streak of bad luck but I hope to pick up before arriving in New York. It is about 10:30 P.M., and I can hear dice rolling above my head. They will probably be at it all night long. Tomorrow is the first day of spring and our ship was commissioned on the same date last year. We are going to celebrate and the Captain is going to speak to us in the morning. And I thank the Lord for guiding us safely through this far. Good night.

March 20, 1945

On this beautiful spring morning we are almost home once again. This is really a big day for all of us aboard ship. Because one year ago today we all went aboard the USS Mason, and she was commissioned and we are celebrating our first anniversary. Everyone is dressed very neatly in their blues and white hats as the morning sun extends her ray of gratitude to make this a perfect day. We received orders to venture into the middle of the convoy to issue instructions to some of the merchant ships, and they were surprised to see Negroes on a war vessel. After we had finished, the Captain delivered his inauguration speech to the crew and it was very nice. At noon we had a delicious dinner with turkey, sweet potatoes, cranberry sauce, dressing, salad, peas, ice cream, cake, candy, nuts, and topped it off with a cigar. I was miserable all afternoon and so was everyone else. We saw two movies during the night and another lovely day has come to an end.

March 21, 1945

We are just one day out of New York and the water is getting rough for the first time today, although it is still quite warm. [unclear] Other than that every one seems to be in pretty good shape. Our section is getting things together to go home on leave and all are anxious to reach New York. The officer I mentioned last week wants to talk to me and I am going to urge him to go thru with his plan, because some one really needs to do something. We will go into Earl, N.J. first to unload depth charges and then pull into New York. Webster has made a bracelet with his and her name stamped on it. I think he really loves her. He has also made his mind up definitely about going home with me. Great deal Mac Neal.

March 22, 1945

Steaming as before, heading for New York. The sea is very rough and it is trying to rain. We are planning on arriving in New York Friday morning if possible. De Cuir isn't feeling so well and might go to the hospital. I think it's his appendix. All of us are hoping that it is warmer in New York this time. We are going into Bayonne New Jersey instead of Brooklyn. It is about a forty-five minute ride to New York. I don't know why they changed but I think something is in the wind about the South Pacific. We just received word that a hurricane is heading our way and we might not be able to make NY before Saturday morning. But we are hoping for the best.

March 23, 1945

I came on duty at twelve o'clock today and it is still bad. Last night was awful. I couldn't sleep a wink last night. The ship really did roll and you couldn't stay in your sack. The convoy has slowed down and we don't really know where we are at present. Our Executive Officer came up and took a sight on the sun and figured out where we were. We are a hundred and twenty-three miles from N.Y. and will get in at six. I talked to the officer today about democracy and he says that we are not being treated fair. He is going to have it investigated and some one is going to be in hot water. He is for us 100%. If we are interviewed we are going to spill everything. They have just called station all anchor details. That means we are going in now. We will go to Earl, New Jersey first to unload ammunition.

> [Dunn wrote the following two entries as if they were letters to him from his wife.]

March 24, 1945

Don't get so excited honey. I know how you feel but you trip over something (smiles). Gee, anyone would think there's no one else on the ship but Dunn, De Cuir, Webb, and Bootsie running in [unclear]. Nevertheless, it makes me feel so damn good to know that my honey is very well liked. I don't think other people could do so well without you (smiles). I can't. One thing I am so glad of, I haven't heard "Mr. Davis" name mentioned throughout this trip and I am so glad he is getting out of your "hair." Here's hoping that's one obstacle that will be forever overcome. I think you are the finest man alive and do thank the "Lord" for bringing you and your friends safely home again. Yours, Jane

March 25, 1945

Well, honey it's my time to crow. Sorry I couldn't make it last night. Now it is getting late and I haven't seen you yet. Gee, I came in early and you forgot to come back. But we still have at least a good week together. Here's hoping Webb will go home with us and will like it. It has really been a lovely day and my trip was [unclear] and tiresome. Now I am starving to death. I am on a diet but I don't want to lose all my weight in one day so hurry home and feed me. Guess the admiral wasn't so lonesome after all or have you been teaching him self-control (smile). I'm keeping my fingers crossed hoping Many and Cook will be there when we get home. I love you very much. Yours, Jane

March 26, 1945

Home on leave for ten days.

8

A Final Trip to Oran

April 3–May 7, 1945

After conducting training exercises, in April the USS Mason *escorted her last convoy to Oran. By this time the final Allied offensive on the Italian front had begun, and an Allied army broke into the Po River valley in mid-April. The* Mason's *crew still wondered if they would be sent to the Pacific, where the war with Japan continued.*

April 3, 1945

Webster and Maxie, his girl friend, were home on leave with us and we had a very nice time. Today I returned and things seem to be the same. Except we have about twenty new men aboard ship and now we are really crowded and don't know where all of them will sleep. Most of the fellows were back from leave and some were A.W.O.L. I slept most of the afternoon while they were bringing stores aboard ship. By the way, Davis and two other boys made Chief [Petty Officer] and you know what will happen now. This afternoon quite a few photographers came aboard and we are going to make a movie this week in Portland, Maine or Conn. Afterwards I guess we will go across with a convoy. We had a movie tonight and later I turned in for the night.

A Final Trip to Oran

April 4, 1945

We pulled out of Bayonne, New Jersey at seven thirty. We are going on a speed run and some of the new boys are seasick already. De Cuir is not back as yet but will be before we leave the states. We might return to New York for the night. We finished putting on ammunition about six o'clock this evening and then got orders to leave. We check out at seven thirty, and a terrific storm is coming up. We ran into it about nine, and I thought that we were out for the count but we finally came out of it. After coming off the bridge Tubby gave my mail to me. I washed up good and retired to my sack reading my mail. And to my surprise I had one letter from Walter Lenear who is in the marines. Then I finally read myself to sleep.

April 5, 1945

This morning the storm is still raging and the fog is so thick that you can't see anything. We are going to Block Island. It is raining and the wind is blowing about fifty miles an hour. At ten o'clock the Captain gave orders to prepare to drop anchor. And at ten thirty we dropped anchor. And now the photographers want to start the picture, but the Captain says to wait awhile. We got orders to get underway immediately for exercises with a submarine. We operated with it all afternoon and then pulled into New London, Conn. But our liberty was up at one o'clock and I couldn't make it to Newport and be back on time. I went on liberty and ran into Suretha Jones, the girl that married Dan Robinson from Charleston. I told them that Jane was in Newport, R.I. After chatting quite awhile I returned to the ship.

April 6, 1945

We came out early this morning for exercises with the sub. It is a very nice day, but cool enough for warm clothing. Most of us are pretty busy with odd jobs here and there with the movie photographers all over the ship. The people of the United States will eventually know about the USS Mason after being in commission for one year. Just before leaving New Jersey one of our gunner's mates tried to miss this next trip by going to the hospital but no dice. So while we were loading ammunition he shot himself in the leg with a .22 pistol and they took him to the hospital. Well, we have finished our exercises for the day, and now we are back in New London for the night.

April 7, 1945

Up early this morning and starting out again with our friendly sub. By the way, this is a submarine base and there are plenty of subs around here. The sun is very bright this morning, but it is still very cool. We operated with the sub all morning and had firing practice ·this afternoon. Pictures were taken all during the day. They caught me sending a message on our large light and I had goggles on. They will probably get shots of us sometime tomorrow. During the night we had battle maneuvers with PT boats and it was very good. We spotted these PT boats as they came into attack and illuminated them with our large 24-inch light. Also our large guns illuminated them [with star shells] at times. We finished at twelve o'clock midnight and proceeded to anchorage for the night.

> [The *Mason*'s War Diary for April 6 records that "official Navy photographers made scenes for a forthcoming Navy motion picture titled 'The Negro Sailor.'"]

April 8, 1945

On this beautiful Sunday morning we are still on the go working with submarines. I slept all of the morning because I had a pretty tough night. The Captain was supposed to hold mast today but I guess he wasn't in the mood for it. There are quite a few boys going before him this time. And I know our friend Chief Davis will be in his glory. Tonight we had another exercise with PT boats, and it lasted for about three hours. The photographers were steadily taking pictures of the event. I received a message from our leader, and it stated that he would leave for Norfolk on Monday at one o'clock. He would leave us in charge of the rest. After we finish exercises tomorrow we will proceed to Norfolk.

April 9, 1945

It is much warmer out this morning, and we are making runs on a submarine so these photographers can get good pictures of us. We finally finished the pictures for this morning and we are now working with the submarine on our exercise. We don't know when we will take the convoy out yet. But all of us are under the impression that it will be to Oran, Algeria, Africa. Our radar went out and we had to return to New London for repairs this evening. All of the officers went ashore early to catch the train for New York. These officers are getting to be no good and I am still not going to take any stuff off of any of them. Our boys went on liberty tonight and they almost had a race riot in New London. Some of the boys got hurt, and the SPs put some in jail. But we will get a break some day.

> [Dunn recalls that DE crews in general were not welcome at New London, which was primarily a submarine base. The racial element added to already existing tensions. "They didn't want a DE, especially if it was black. New London was alright. It was not the people, it was the [submarine] crews." Dunn says that the *Mason's* captain warned his men to "be careful when you go out."]

April 10, 1945

This morning we got underway at six thirty to complete our exercises but the fog was so thick that we had to drop anchor for the morning. We didn't get underway again until one o'clock. We were supposed to shoot at a target towed by an airplane but the fog settled again and we couldn't fire. So we finally gave up the idea and started for Norfolk, Va. It is still foggy and we had three small ships including a destroyer, and we are in charge of them all. This is something very unusual. All of us aboard ship are not satisfied at all. It doesn't seem like a war vessel at all but like a kindergarten. They don't think about the feelings of a man but just of themselves. But something is bound to break sooner or later.

April 11, 1945

It is very foggy this morning and I came on watch at four o'clock this morning. We are now entering the channel going into Norfolk. We really hate to go into this place because it is a bad liberty town, and some of the boys might get into trouble due to segregation on the ferries and other places. We pulled into the pier at 12:00 A.M., and of course all eyes were on the Mason. The liberty was granted at 2:30 P.M.; Webster, Luster [Roosevelt Luster], Purce [Howard W. Purce], and myself went out together to see Mrs. Johnson in Portsmouth, Va. Instead of finding her at home we found [unclear] which was a surprise. So we talked and had a few drinks and later went for a ride in her car to Newport at a club and then returned to the ship.

April 12, 1945

It is very foggy here this morning but it usually gets clear about ten o'clock and turns out to be a very nice day. Last night we were supposed to be back at midnight but didn't make it until six this morning. The transportation is so bad around here. Webster and Purce were caught, but Luster got by. They were restricted and will go up to Captain's mast at sea. We were supposed to leave this evening but got a 24-hour delay in our orders, so I went on liberty and

A Final Trip to Oran

called Mrs. Johnson and said good bye to her. Later, I found the club which Kinkle Spencer and another boy that went to W. Va. State College were running and they were glad to see me. We talked of old times at state, had some drinks, and I got back to the ship on time.

April 13, 1945

It is foggy again this morning but it is quite warm. We fell into quarters for muster (roll call) and later everyone seemed to be busy. We cleaned our signal bridge which only took one hour. After finishing we just sat around watching the other ships. Across from us are two large cruisers, Chicago and Augusta. We talked to some of the boys with our signal flags and they invited us over to look over their ship. They have a band aboard which plays every day from 12:30 until 1:00 P.M. At three o'clock we got underway. We anchored in the Chesapeake Bay outside of Norfolk to pick up our convoy in the morning. It will probably take us about sixteen days to go across. So we are off to the races again.

April 14, 1945

On this beautiful morning we lifted anchor and got underway at five thirty. There are a lot of ships forming and all are merchant ships. I have just about been up all night and they are keeping us busy sending messages. Our ship is next to the senior ship of the convoy and she keeps busy at all times. This afternoon we have to deliver instructions to seventeen merchant ships, and it will take us some time to finish it. Our destination is still unknown. Webb is trying to talk the man out of doing the [captain's] mast, and he has just about talked a hole in our executive officer's head. But I am quite sure that he will beat the rap. Well, we are still busy and I shall retire after finishing our work.

105

April 15, 1945

I was just thinking two Sundays ago I was home and what a difference two weeks can make in a sailor's life. It is a very gloomy Sunday at sea today. There are dark clouds everywhere and it has been raining. But it is very warm. The fresh air really smells good blowing on your face. We are headed for the Mediterranean Sea and it will be much warmer. No excitement has come up as yet, but we are looking for a lot of it this time. There are two German submarines hanging around somewhere out there. The boys seem to be in a good spirits. I guess it is the spring fever. We had a movie this afternoon and will have another tonight.

April 16, 1945

Our ship is guarding the rear of the convoy but will change each day. It's very beautiful out today with the sun beaming down and the water just as blue as the sky. There is really not much to say on these trips because it is practically the same routine. But we are kept much busier than usual. Although we do amuse ourselves listening to all the latest records aboard ship. I have actually read more since I have been on this ship than I have in my life. We are not in the danger sector as yet, but there are still lurking subs to be found and we have to be very careful. We will probably hit the Azores next week sometime and then the trouble will start.

April 17, 1945

This is a lovely spring morning but there are no birds or trees, just sky and water. Frank Sinatra is singing "I Dream of You," and you can see the thought of each man by the expression on his face. These boys are hard, rugged, but they can be touched at times by a little sentiment. Our welfare officer is having each man write something about his hobbies, where he was working before entering the Navy, and the school he attended. He is going to send it to our

"Cruiser" Johnson enjoys a smoke near gun no. 21. Courtesy of James Graham.

hometown paper. Today we received orders to pass more mail to ships in the convoy. As we did this, the merchant marines looked at us as if to say, "where did they come from?" And we get a kick out of telling them what to do. (Bonjour Madamoselle, Good-by Madam)

April 18, 1945

We are steaming as before on this lovely spring morning about 1,000 miles out to sea. Everyone seems to be in a good mood here of late. Maybe it's the spring in the air. We are spring cleaning this week and getting everything in good shape. All of us miss De Cuir and Jimmy, but I'm sure they will be with us on the next trip. We usually have an open forum during our chows, and some of the things you hear are a knock out. The single boys usually talk about each other while the married fellows sit back and agitate an argument between the other fellows. There are never any fights and the fellows really enjoy themselves.

April 19, 1945

Everyone is up on these beautiful spring mornings, standing on deck breathing the pure fresh air into their lungs. I know we daydream most of the day and night thinking of our loved ones. The nights are really beautiful, it's like a Midsummer Night's Dream. We are all hoping that the war in Germany is over by the time we get back to the states. Today Luster was painting the deck and he said to me, "Don't you ever work?" I said, "Why I worked for Carnegie Illinois Steel Corp., 8 hours a day and that was enough to last the white man a long time." Well, I seem to be in the way around here, so I guess that I will take a shower and shave. I must keep sharp for the mermaids (smile). Our destination is Oran, Africa, the beautiful Arabian Nights. "Wow."

April 20, 1945

This morning everyone was early. We have to get sleeping quarters and other places ready for inspection this afternoon. Of course, you see a lot of the boys shirking their work, but the boys usually find where one is hiding. I helped on the signal bridge this morning. There is never a lot of work to be done there because we usually keep it in good shape. I went on watch at noon and the boss of the convoy had a sub contact but didn't find anything. We were to hold our inspection at 2:00 P.M., but it was held up for an hour because of another sub attack. At 3:00 P.M. inspection started and didn't finish until 6:00 P.M. Everything was in good shape.

A Final Trip to Oran

April 21, 1945

The sun was very beautiful coming up on the horizon this morning. Later on this morning it got cloudy and it looks like rain. I have been sleeping all morning and woke up just in time for noon chow and the BS-session in the chow hall. Some of the boys have found out from girls after making them half drunk that some of the boys are eating [unclear] and they light right in on the boys as soon as they hit the chow hall. The boys accused don't even deny it. One never knows, does one? After finishing chow this evening I went on watch and several of the boys came up to keep my company. We talked of different things and different people. And soon I had stood my four hours.

Dear Jane,

I miss you so much, Darling, but I try to keep myself busy doing something to keep from thinking of you too much. I am about halfway across the Atlantic and I have been doing pretty good so far. I sit around and listen to sad stories from some of the boys about their wives. They are wondering whether they are loyal to them. But that is the least of my worries. I always did trust you. Well, the admiral and I are fine, although when he thinks about you, he loses all control and I have to talk to him. Otherwise he is OK. He also has plenty of self-control. You won't have to worry, darling. You will probably lose a lot of weight when I get back because I am going to try and see every night. Love you very much.

April 22, 1945

It is nice and clear out this morning and the fresh air smells good. As usual we have hot cakes and bacon for morning chow. I am getting so fat I don't know what to do. My stomach is really getting large. I sat on the signal bridge all morning and I guess that I was dreaming most of the time while watching the sun and the

109

enchanting waters. I am such a sucker for beautiful scenery. We received a message yesterday to be prepared for a change at any time. And that all ships in the Atlantic would be transferred to the South Pacific. Make all necessary repairs while in New York. We knew that it would come sooner or later.

April 23, 1945

The water is a little rough this morning but it is very pretty out. At twelve noon we will be passing some of the islands in the Azores and that means that we are more than half way across. We were called to general quarters just a little ago for firing practice. Balloons were thrown into the water for targets. All the guns were fired and the boys did quite well. At 1:00 P.M. we began a flag hoist drill in which he designated one of the other escorts to lead. The [unclear] hoisted a signal and we followed suit. The boss sent us a message saying that the hoist was wrong. We referred them to the Navy call book and they still can't find it. So the leading ship said to skip it. After we had finished the boss sent us another message, apologizing and thanked us for correcting them. Small world, isn't it?

April 24, 1945

This really is a beautiful morning, and I am on watch. The Boss sent me a challenge by light and tried to catch me off guard but I was right on him like white on rice. Our communications officer walks around very proud, knowing that he has four signalmen who can match wits with anyone. Some of the boys are washing their hammocks today. And I imagine that we will have another inspection Friday. We are only six days out of Oran, Algeria. Well, it is time for another flag hoist drill, so I must go. Well, our flag hoist didn't go so good today because of the sun. I slept the other half of the afternoon. Tonight is very beautiful. The stars are bright; the sky is clear and the moon is shining like a large street light, lighting up everything. But to bed I must go.

A Final Trip to Oran

April 25, 1945

I've never seen such a beautiful day. I was topside all of the morning. Some of the boys were after me about walking around with my shoes shined and sitting down while they were working. They called me the pimp of the ship which I resented right away. Last night I think just about everybody on board was seasick. That moon really did something to you. To top that off, Purce and I were listening to the program on the radio coming from New York. The orchestra was playing "Don't You Know I Care," and it really did send us. Our division officer just took the history of our life and is going to send it to each of our hometowns. I gave him the Daily Mail and Gazette. We have some good movies aboard so I am standing by. We will reach Africa Sunday.

April 26, 1945

We are still having these lovely days as we near our destination. Everyone seems to be in a very good mood. We haven't had a general alarm as yet but we never know what minute a sub will attack. A destroyer was sunk and an aircraft carrier was hit just outside of Norfolk Monday night. We had our flag hoist drill as usual today. The Boss said it was well handled. Last night I saw "Here Come the Waves," with Betty Hutton, Bing Crosby and Sunny Tufts. All of us enjoyed it very much. I think that we will have another inspection tomorrow. Because I can see some of the boys cleaning a little more than usual. "Africa or Bust"

[Navy records show that no destroyer or destroyer escort was sunk in the Atlantic in April 1945.]

April 27, 1945

Steaming as before and still no alarm as yet. But we have our fingers crossed. It is a bright sunny day and this fresh air just brings the gypsy out in you. Today we are having inspection and all of the boys are turning to. After noon chow our flag hoist drill commenced and we did very well. The Captain inspected the signal bridge first of all and found it to be in very good shape. We also had a payday today, but I didn't draw any money. I will wait until I get back to the states. I know the boys will be gambling and I am not going to take any chance on getting broke. Our destination is near and we should hit Gibraltar by noon tomorrow and Oran Sunday morning. The ship's service has now opened and I must get some cigarettes.

April 28, 1945

I was on watch this morning from 0400 until 0800 and I have never seen anything as beautiful as the sunrise. Everyone was just standing and staring at the beautiful celestial body. After having my morning chow I slept all morning. During the afternoon we did the usual thing. At six o'clock we reached the Straits of Gibraltar. A submarine came in on one side of the convoy and several ships dropped depth charges. Even Navy blimps and planes came in for the attack and sank it. After all of the ships were inside everything was safe. All ships turned their lights on. If you ever want to see something beautiful one should see the moon on the Mediterranean at night. It really brings your love down. It is now 2:30, so good-night.

April 29, 1945

After such a terrific dream last night, I awakened to find a beautiful morning sun coming up over the mountain. I just sat and watched it all day. We were in charge of our group and it is amazing when you think of Negroes leading a couple of white ships around and telling them what to do. We arrived in Oran about three o'clock this afternoon, and the other American ships just stared at us as we pulled in. Of course, you could imagine what they were saying, but we didn't mind because we knew that we were great. We finally tied up and some of the boys went on liberty. I had the duty so some of us played basketball until dark and then saw a movie. We see one every night. Later showered down and hit my sack.

[The *Mason's* War Diary for April 28 observed, "The Oran area provides excellent recreational facilities for enlisted men."]

April 30, 1945

It is nice and cool this morning, but about ten o'clock it really gets hot. Most of the fellows are working this morning but my boys and me stayed on the signal bridge all morning. After the noon chow we played basketball and really enjoyed the exercise. The water is so pretty and green that it makes you want to jump right in. But one never knows what's in there. Around three o'clock Bootsie, Purce and myself went on liberty and had a few drinks but didn't buy any souvenirs. One of the boys took pictures and later we returned to the ship. Liberty is up at ten o'clock and it doesn't get dark until after ten. God bless America.

May 1, 1945

At seven thirty this P.M. we went out into the blue Mediterranean for firing practice. We saw turtles in the water as large as a person's head. We are always talking about what we would be doing with our wives or girl friends if we were in the states. We really miss the bone, because that is something of the past. Our group stayed out until about three o'clock. And we just about shot away the target and the Captain was very pleased. Webb and I pulled a little business deal and made a little cash. After we had tied up, most of us played basketball until dark which is about ten. And then the movie began. So I am turning in for the night.

Charles T. Kelley, a radioman on the *Mason*, on
shore near Oran. Courtesy of James Graham.

May 2, 1945

It is quite windy in Oran today and we are getting underway this
A.M. for firing practice just outside the harbor. The sun is out this
morning but it is a little cool. We operated with a friendly sub until
noon. The sea tossed us around so much that we had to come in.
After we had gotten in our division went on a beer party. We had
plenty of sandwiches and beer. We played softball and had a very
nice time. We returned to the ship about seven thirty and some of
the boys played basketball. It doesn't get dark until about ten
thirty. Later I went to the movie and saw "Frenchman's Creek"
and then turned in for the night.

A Final Trip to Oran

May 3, 1945

We are not going out this morning because we are having person-nel inspection in whites. At nine thirty the Captain inspected us, and our division was the best of all. At ten thirty we had a flaghoist drill and finished at eleven fifteen. Two other divisions went on a recreation party at noon. They took beer and sandwiches. After eating chow the rest of us aboard played basketball. I had liberty but I didn't go. Webb and Bootsie went together. I stood a watch for one of the boys and didn't go on liberty. There isn't anything much to do in Oran except to get a few drinks. I went to the movie and saw a very good movie: "Mrs. Parkington," with Walter Pidgeon and Greer Garson. Afterwards I turned in.

May 4, 1945

We are just lounging around today. There isn't very much to be done. In fact I don't have anything to do. It's a very beautiful day and the boys are playing ball all around the harbor. The town itself is very quiet. The name of this town is Mers El Kebir and it is about six miles from Oran. Today another group of fellows went on the recreation party. They also carried quite a few cases of beer and many sandwiches. Most of us don't mind being over here a week this time because the recreation helps to keep your mind occupied. You also see very good movies at night.

Dear Jane,

I've been sitting around thinking an awful lot. I know that you have always loved me. But you were just like a sparrow that had to be taught to fly. You also know that I loved you. There were two parts of me. One part that you loved and another that you forgave. I loved to travel and see different things. I was full of excitement. This is the part that you loved. On the other hand I was just a scoundrel but you always forgave that part of me. But you have

115

fought and will hang on to me forever and I do admire your spunk. It always summed to one thing. I am always ending up with you. I have always loved you and always will. You are a darling. This might sound a little fantastic but it is true.

May 5, 1945

On this beautiful morning I was awakened earlier than usual. They put me in charge of a working party of ten men. We left the ship at eight thirty and reported to the destroyer club. The place had to be cleaned. I had the boys to clean the place. After we had finished, the officer gave us a case of beer. We returned to ship. Now we are getting ready to go on another beer party. Webb's division has challenged us to a softball game. At two o'clock we left the ship for our outing. After we had gotten organized the feud was on. But Webb's team beat us. Bootsie starred. Later we drank all of the beer and finished eating the sandwiches. After returning to the ship we proceeded to play basketball. What a day.

> [Dunn recalls that he and his men volunteered to clean the club on shore, anticipating that they would receive some beer. He does not remember this as an instance of discrimination.]

May 6, 1945

There is no wind stirring at all this morning and the sun is really coming down. Everybody has their white uniforms on this morning. Some of the boys are sore from playing ball yesterday. But I feel like a million. Bootsie and I surprised the boys. It appeared that I was much faster than they had expected me to be. I was at my same old position on first base. Bootsie really roamed the outfield. At ten o'clock about 15 of us went to church and took holy communion. And we had a very nice service this morning. Bootsie and several other boys went on liberty to get our last few drinks this evening. It was really hot. We returned to the ship early and saw a movie. Went swimming in the Mediterranean.

May 7, 1945

We are making all preparations for getting underway this morning. All of us are very happy to be going home once again. Our convoy has lined up and is ready to shove off. It's a lovely day to start our trip back to the states. I came back to my sack and slept all morning until chow time. After chow several of us played pinochle until it was time to go on watch. We went on watch at four o'clock and received about four messages. One of them said to guard all radio frequencies. About six o'clock we received word that Germany had surrendered and were glad to hear it. The subs out there in the Atlantic are supposed to surrender by radio and that's why we have to guard all frequencies. And now I will turn in for the night.

9

Coming Home at Last

May 8–23, 1945

Germany surrendered on May 8, 1945, V-E Day (Victory in Europe Day). All submarines were ordered to surface and proceed to the nearest European port. On May 28, 1945, the sea war in the Atlantic, Indian, and Arctic Oceans officially ended with the announcement that merchant ships no longer needed to travel in armed convoys. By this time German submarines, surface raiders, and bombers had sunk about 3,500 Allied ships, killing 45,000 merchant seamen. On the German side, 28,000 sailors lost their lives, and 784 submarines were sunk—70 percent of the German submarine force.

With the war in Europe over, the Mason *returned home. Coming back to their wives, girlfriends, and families, the men put most of their tensions behind them. They continued to wonder, however, if they would be sent to the war in the Pacific.*

May 8, 1945

Our convoy is moving very slowly this morning because other ships are joining us in Gibraltar. I have nothing much to do on watch this morning so I am making a pair of semaphore flags for my personal use. At noon we began to pass the rock of Gibraltar, and several ships joined us. Several of these ships were full dressed celebrating V.E. Day. We all wished that we were in New York to-day. Two hospital ships passed us heading for the United States. There hasn't been any scuttlebutt about where we might go as yet. But I imagine we will pick up on it very soon. We are now going out of the Straits of Gibraltar and should arrive in New York in about fifteen days.

May 9, 1945

Well, the war is over! Germany has capitulated and Japan is suing for peace. By the way, Dyson thought this up. All of the boys seem to be in a good mood on this beautiful morning. Most of us have been asleep. It seems as though we might have a little excitement before arriving in the states. The Boss of the convoy told us to be prepared to board a submarine. All German subs are to surface and surrender. The Captain has taken one or two boys out of each division. Webb was one of the boys. Webb told the Captain that Dyson could speak German and they added his name to the list. We are all hoping that we run into one. I would like to have a German flag.

[The *Mason's* War Diary for May 8 recorded, "Prize crew further organized and trained for boarding surrendered German submarines."]

May 10, 1945

The wind is very strong today and the sea is tossing us around like a rubber ball. I was on watch this morning and the sprays came up on the signal bridge. Dyson is still giving Webb down the country about tricking him. He swears that he is going to get even with him. They had firing practice for the boys going on boarding parties. You would have laughed yourself sick watching Webb shoot a forty-five. He has grown his beard again. It is going to be good if we should run across a submarine. I am looking for one of them to kill some Germans.

119

CHAPTER 9

May 11, 1945

Today is cloudy and very dreary looking. All of the boys are getting ready for the Captain's inspection. My detail is on the signal bridge and I don't have anything to do. The boys are now cleaning in our compartment, and some of them are dodging Tubby. He is a signalman in charge of the boys. After watching Tubby work so hard, I decided to give him a hand. I swept out our compartment and happened to look and found one of the boys yelling to the others. He said that we should remember three dates that are important for 1945. The President died on April 13, the European war was over on May 9, and Dunn was seen with a broom in his hand on May 11. The Captain made his rounds and found the ship in fairly good shape. Afterwards all retired.

May 12, 1945

This is a much better day. The sun is shining but it is a little windy. After morning chow I was just about to retire when Snafu [DuFau] came down and said our communications officer wanted us to wash the signal flags. Well, we began to curse him out, of course to ourselves. There are 142 flags. We picked out about 24 flags and began our task. One of the boys saw me working and called about twenty guys and they really did ride us, because we never have to do very much. They had their fun today, but we still didn't wash all of them and never will. That was my last job for quite a while. And I'm not kidding.

May 13, 1945

This is really an ideal Mothers Day. The sky is clear with a few clouds here and there. And the sun is shining its extravagant rays upon the Blue Atlantic. Nature is grand. Everyone is taking it easy today. I just shaved and had a nice hot and cold shower. Our noon chow was fairly good. Chicken, sweet potatoes, dressing, asparagus, soup, and cake. Music is heard throughout the ship. It gets under your skin, but that's the life of a sailor. There is also a movie going on this afternoon but I am on watch but I guess that it will be shown again tonight. Denson has done pretty good on this trip. He has learned to play pinochle and that keeps his mind occupied most of the time. We should arrive on the 22nd of May.

May 14, 1945

We are steadily steaming towards New York and it really is a good feeling when you are going home. It's another fine day and the fresh air makes one feel very good. The ship is getting another good painting since the weather is so nice, and we don't have to worry about submarines. All of us are busy doing something. I am making a bracelet for my sugar and so are some of the other fellows for their loved ones. They started that damn flaghoist drill again but we don't mind it so much on our way home. Everybody is trying to think of some way to keep from going to the South Pacific. But we will know soon. I have my fingers crossed.

May 15, 1945

Steaming as before, and everybody seems to be very happy and contented. But one never knows, does one? Our food is getting low but we can make it home. Twenty-seven submarines have given up in the Atlantic and there still are some around. We didn't realize there were so many still in the Atlantic. I just guess we were over the average lucky. But that luck is bound to leave us some time. That's why we want to get off here. I asked my division officer for a transfer today and he wanted to know why I wanted off. So I told him that I was tired of the water. He says, "I'll see what I can do for you." Bootsie is still winning all of the pinochle games and money.

May 16, 1945

On this beautiful morning we are still screening the convoy. We have just finished chow and the deck force is washing down the deck. The boys in the C-division never have very much to do during the day unless an inspection is due on Friday. Most of us have been lolly gagging about the ship playing pinochle or arguing about some school. Sometimes they talk about the boy's girl friend or wife. They will say that Jowdy is probably taking over while you are at sea. But I don't enter into these discussions. Although I agitate. I finally finished the bracelet for my wife. I am sure that she will like it. Nothing of importance has happened today so I will attend the movie and then turn in.

May 17, 1945

I was up at six this morning. I took a nice hot and cold shower and then had bacon & eggs and pineapple juice for chow. The boys asked me what I knew. We are having an inspection tomorrow and I am going to give the boys a hand on the signal bridge. In fact I have the duty. We finished in a short while. Our division officer wanted us to hang over the side of the bridge and clean it. But we refused and I don't know what the outcome will be. He didn't say any more about it. Townsend got a hold of it and started to agitate in the chow hall. We couldn't do it now. Everything is still quiet aboard ship. The boys say that Webb is just like a black jew. He is selling bracelets. The day has come to an end and the sun has just set in the west. So I will see another movie.

May 18, 1945

Today is inspection and everybody is up early. It is beautiful today and the sea is calm and blue, and the sky is very clear. Webb had his usual argument with the boys at chow this morning and they can't get the best of him. But Dyson can shut him up by mentioning

Maxie's name. Says he is going to marry her this trip in. We put the finishing touches on the signal bridge this morning. Our officer hasn't said anything as yet. Bootsie just finished beating Gibson and myself playing pinochle. Inspection started at 2:00 P.M. And the Captain said it was excellent. So he says tomorrow is a holiday. We went into the convoy to deliver mail and the patty boys just looked at us and wondered. I am sitting on the signal bridge on watch. It is 7:05 P.M. and the sun is going down and I am imagining everything.

May 19, 1945

Steaming as before in company with seven escorts and forty merchant ships en route to the United States, speed 11 knots and we are holding down position five. Standard speed fifteen knots. The weather is a little cloudy and the sea is rough. The crew was paid off this morning and I am trying to collect some of my money the boys owe me. One should really see Webb going around with his [unclear] black book. When I last saw him he had a hand full of money. The boys were gambling all afternoon and I am trying to make up my mind whether to or not. I went on watch at eight tonight and the big poker game was going on below. But at 12:00 when I came down one of the Chiefs had just about broke some of the boys.

May 20, 1945

We are only about two days out of New York and the water is rough this morning. My friend Snafu won one hundred and three dollars in a crap game yesterday. You can hear the water coming over the deck of the ship above and one has to be very careful while walking on topside. We had a very nice noon chow with fried chicken. Later we sat around and played cards. This storm has held us back for an extra day. But we should be in Wednesday at midnight. A few of the boys owe me but don't have any money. But I'll

123

get it somehow. You have to hold on to something if you don't want to get thrown all over the ship. It is very rough.

May 21, 1945

This morning is just about as bad as yesterday. I didn't get any sleep at all last night. In fact I had to get up. Bootsie and several others and myself played cards just about all day. The boys got me for a few dollars. I should be able to get it back before entering port. Our chow today was pretty bad. They served beef and we all hate it. The convoy is splitting up tomorrow and I think that we are taking some of the ships to Norfolk. Afterwards we are going to race one of the other escorts into New York. One of our officers made a bet. I think we should win. Well, it's time for me to go on watch.

May 22, 1945

It's a world of difference out today. The sea has calmed down quite a bit. The convoy has split up and we are on our way into Norfolk. We sat around and played poker all morning until several of us had to go on watch at noon. I won my money back this morning including a few extra dollars. There wasn't anything to do on watch this afternoon. I only received one message. So, I just stretched out and took a sun bath. It is good for the muscles. Webb is really doing OK with his little business. He has the boys running after him for bracelets. But he manages to get around to all of them. Pipe down, turn in your bunks. Smoking light is out in berthing spaces. All lights out. Good night.

May 23, 1945

I came on watch this morning at four o'clock and the weather is fairly nice. We are now going into the channel of Norfolk. As soon

At the Mandalay in 1945 (from left to right): George Polk and his girlfriend, Jane and James Dunn, and Howard Purce and his girlfriend. Courtesy of James A. Dunn.

as the escorts come out to meet the convoy, we are heading for New York and should get in tonight. Our engines will be wide open all the way. This is really a beautiful day at sea. We have left the other two ships with us. We are now passing Atlantic City, and the boys are all shining their shoes and getting ready for liberty tonight. The sun is going down and night will soon fall. Most of the boys are topside and patiently waiting. Well we are now pulling in and it's eleven thirty. It is really good to be back again. I am on my way to Mandalay.

Afterword

On Land

Dunn returned to the USS *Mason* for training exercises, but the ship was not sent to the Pacific. Decommissioned on October 16, 1945, the *Mason* was scrapped in 1947. Dunn and his wife returned to Charleston, West Virginia, where his mother lived. After going back to work at the Carnegie Steel plant for a short time, Dunn attended West Virginia State College on the G.I. bill. There he received training in drafting and in masonry and bricklaying. However, he found that American life remained segregated and that discrimination against African Americans was still the norm. Most bricklaying jobs in Charleston were controlled by unions, and, as Dunn says, "we could not get into the union."

Seeking better opportunities, Dunn and his family moved back to Columbus, Ohio. Although racism and discrimination on the part of union members continued to be a problem, he was able to get some bricklaying jobs. The winters were cold, however, and Dunn sought work indoors. He eventually secured a position in inventory control for a large Defense Department depot, and in 1976 received a "special achievement" award for the superior quality of his work there. Meanwhile, his wife worked in a dress shop in downtown Columbus. Together they reared a son and daughter, James Jr. and Muriel. Dunn retired in 1979, and he and his wife continue to live in Columbus.

The efforts of James A. Dunn and other African Americans in the armed forces during World War II—the Tuskegee airmen, tank

127

James A. Dunn in retirement in the early 1980s.
Courtesy of James A. Dunn.

commanders in George Patton's army, and others—paved the way
for desegregation in America's military. In 1948 President Harry S
Truman issued an order desegregating the armed forces, thus con-
tributing to a civil rights movement that changed the face of the
nation.

Bibliographic Note

James A Dunn's diary now resides in the Rare Book Room of The Ohio State University Library in Columbus, Ohio, kindly donated by James A. Dunn Jr. A copy of the diary may be found in the archives and library of the Ohio History Connection (formerly the Ohio Historical Society) in Columbus, Ohio. I conducted tape-recorded interviews with Dunn on April 6 and 8, June 2, and July 31, 1995; copies of the tapes along with partial transcripts of them are available at the Ohio History Connection's archives and library. The USS *Mason*'s War Diary, Commodore Alfred Lind's report on Convoy N.Y. 119, and Captain William Blackford's letters are available at the Naval Historical Center in the Washington Navy Yard in Washington, DC. The *Mason*'s daily log is available in the National Archives in Washington, DC. There are two books dealing with the activities of the *Mason*: Mary Pat Kelly, *Proudly We Served: The Men of the USS* Mason (Annapolis: Naval Institute Press, 1995) and Charles Dana Gibson, *Ordeal of Convoy N.Y. 119* (New York: South Street Seaport Museum, 1973).

Accounts of naval warfare in the Atlantic include Samuel Eliot Morrison, *The Atlantic Battle Won, May 1943–May 1945* (Edison, NJ: Castle Books, 1956); Robert F. Cross, *Shepherds of the Sea: Destroyer Escorts in World War II* (Annapolis: Naval Institute Press, 2010); Gordon Williamson, *U-Boats Vs Destroyer Escorts: The Battle of the Atlantic* (Oxford, UK: Osprey Publishing, 2007); and V. E. Tarrant, *The Last Year of the Kriegsmarine, May 1944–May 1945* (London: Arms & Armour Press, 1996). On African Americans in the navy, see James Baker Farr, *Black Odyssey: The Seafaring Traditions of Afro Americans* (New York: Peter Lang, 1991); Eric Purdon, *Black Company: The Story of Subchaser 1264* (Washington, DC: R. B. Luce, 1972); and Paul Stilwell, ed., *The Golden Thirteen: Recollections of the First Black Naval Officers* (Annapolis: Naval Institute Press, 1993).